Garbage Theology

Garbage Theology

The Unseen World of Waste and What It Means for the Salvation of Every Person, Every Place, and Every Thing

CALEB CRAY HAYNES

McGahan

Garbage Theology: The Unseen World of Waste and What It Means for the Salvation of Every Person, Every Place, and Every Thing

Copyright © 2021 by Caleb Cray Haynes

McGahan Publishing House | Lynchburg, Tennessee
www.mphbooks.com
Requests for information should be sent to:
info@mphbooks.com

ISBN 978-1-951252-16-8 (Paperback)

ISBN 978-1-951252-17-5 (eBook)

Library of Congress Control Number: 2021945897

"Caleb's passion, experiences, and hope are compelling. *Garbage Theology* is a practical tool both for those who want to learn where and how to begin the journey and those who wish to deepen their understanding of the subject. It is a compelling reminder that participation in the life and mission of God is holistic; it includes striving to steward well God's creation."
Dr. Filimão M. Chambo, General Superintendent in the Church of the Nazarene

"*Garbage Theology* is the best book ever written on our overconsumption and how our lifestyle harms God's beautiful creation. Bi-vocational Garbage-man Pastor Caleb Cray Haynes opened my eyes to wonderful biblical insights on waste, destruction, and renewal for our common home and our relationship with its Creator. With honest humor that is also troubling, Garbage Theology overturns poor biblical understanding with correct Biblical truth for defending God's creation."
Rev. Mitch Hescox. President/C.E.O., The Evangelical Environmental Network and co-author of *Caring For Creation: The Evangelicals Guide to Climate Change and Healthy Environment*

"If you intend to live in ease and comfort, you won't read this book. But if you love your neighbor, and are willing to imagine what that looks like in practice, you will open yourself to new ways of thinking about trash, consumption, and simplicity. This book messed with my ease and I predict it might do the same for you."
Dan Boone. President, Trevecca Nazarene University

"*Garbage Theology* is anything but! Full of Scriptural insights and practical applications, *Garbage Theology* is a must-read for anyone concerned about God's glorious creation and the health of future generations. Told from an unusual (if not unique!) perspective of a clergy-garbage collector, Pastor Haynes makes a convicting case for focusing less on stuff and more on treasures that will never rust, ruin, or rot."
Matthew Sleeth, MD. Executive Director of Blessed Earth and author of various books on Christianity and the environment

"From the get-go this book captures the imagination, forces deep questions, teases us into surprising places of agreement, reshapes our thinking and offers challenges to our lives and solutions - things we <u>can</u> do. In a readable way the pastoral heart of Rev. Haynes pushes

us towards being a healing people: our relationship with possessions, the Earth, lands, places, ourselves, our values and our ideas all come under the gaze of someone who communicates creation care with passion and wisdom and pushes us to become part of God's healing of the world. Rooted in Scripture and vibrant with integrity, the book takes us a journey through global and local spaces - calling us personally and collectively to a new way of life, and a new way of being church. Each chapter is researched well, and then leaps into reflection and action that can be done as an individual or as a small group - together we can make a difference and bear witness to God's goodness and love for the world. Thankfully, Garbage Theology made me sense that I too could be part of God's hope breaking out on Earth as it does in heaven."
Deirdre Brower Latz. Principal of Nazarene Theological College

"Garbage Theology is far more than a treatise on how we can reduce waste and care for creation, which would be a worthy goal in itself. Rev. Caleb Haynes lays out a clear theological foundation, amplified by scientific data and real-world experience, for reframing our relationship with things, people, culture, and ultimately, God. The practices contained in this book are deeply spiritual, practical, and most importantly, doable. Learning to be responsible stewards of the Earth, and the people living in it is not only a way to preserve our God-given home, but also an opportunity to bear witness to the ongoing redemptive work of Christ in the world. This book is a vital resource that comes at just the right time."
Albert Hung. District Superintendent, Northern California District Church of the Nazarene

From my earliest days I was taught that the Earth was a gift of God and was to be cherished and protected. Our family vacationed by camping in the mountains, on the coast, and in great forests. Dad was a Nazarene pastor who loved the out of doors, especially sensing the presence of God in the beauty of nature. Dad insisted that holiness of heart led, among many other expressions, to care for God's good Earth, for the sake of everyone. This book challenges me to recall, and to reclaim, one of the essential expressions of what it means to be holy. I love the book and its premise. It seems to capture what I believe so deeply: Care for creation is an act of worship.
Jesse C. Middendorf. NTS Executive Director of the Center for Pastoral Leadership & General Superintendent Emeritus in the Church of the Nazarene.

Contents

Germinations

To my **Gran**,
Who first showed me how to put my hands
into the dirt.
&
To my two little **Girls**,
Who will inherit the Earth.

Acknowledgments

There isn't a story that stands alone. Every story is interwoven with the daily lives of many many others and this book is a testament to that. I am so thankful for all the stories that have helped shape my own. There aren't enough pages to thank all of the lives that have helped birth this one.

I am exceptionally thankful for my amazing wife, Emily. If I've managed to produce anything good in life, she's been there loving, dreaming, laboring alongside me in it. She is a loving force in the world who invites everyone she encounters into growth. Without her support, this book would not exist.

I am so thankful for my community, Kaleo, who continually teaches me what it means to follow Jesus with others in all of the beauty and struggle of life. For Ryan, who is a friend beyond what anyone deserves... who trusted me enough to drive his truck around Nashville for years, working together with me to change the world one load at a time. For Jason, who always seems to draw me further into the mystery of being a keeper of this Earth we call home while sharing a vision for a hopeful tomorrow. For friends such as David, who shared the hard work of hauling with me and gladly jumps into dumpsters with me still today. I'm so thankful for my family for always loving and supporting me no matter what, this work wouldn't be here without them. And for everyone who kept inquiring about this book along the way and helped me remember what all this is for, thank you!

In the end, I'm grateful to a God who created us and has given us this chance to write these stories and weave them together and who can work even through pages such as these for restoration and healing of the world.

Introduction

If you would have told me ten years ago that I would be writing a book on waste one day, I would have laughed! Unsuspectingly, the work I began one day as someone loading and hauling trash, work that I strongly disliked in the beginning, became the necessary vehicle for learning about the breadth, length, height, and depth of the love of God. Education teaches you many things, pastoring a church teaches you an entirely new set of things, and, as it happens, picking up trash for years on end becomes yet another teacher. We are generally comfortable with reflecting on the expanse of the universe to speak of the expansiveness of God. We are familiar with looking at the stories of miracles and great acts of kindness to help us grasp the greatness of God. However, I would like to propose here that studying the "mundane" pieces of creation may have just as much to teach us about how great and expansive God's all-encompassing presence is. Even further, how might that which we have discarded, disdained, rejected, and wasted as a society inform us about ourselves, and thus about the fingerprint of God in our own lives?

This book is about seeing. If you could peer into the intersection of how you consume and what you believe about God, would you do it? It may not be a beautiful sight or an easy conversation, because the choices we make every single day can bring about invisible horrors or pieces of heaven. The pages that follow tell the story, detailing all the ways in which our waste is hidden from us and the kind of posture that produces waste in the first place. So, will you take this opportunity to see it?

To read this book may require nothing from you at the outset. You may absorb these pages and gently nod your head with a "mmhmm." Yet for some, reading these pages may require much more from you, especially if this is a new way of seeing. Yet the same challenge (or opportunity) lies ahead for all readers and anyone willing to grow openness.

It seems quite audacious to write a book full of words that you believe someone else ought to read. That is unless we understand that each of us possesses something that the other needs. We are an almost 8 billion wide collective voice, and no one holds the entire pie. Openness is about understanding that you have not arrived but are arriving. Openness is the willingness to unlearn so that you might re-learn. Openness invites everyone to be your teacher. Even the garbage and the garbage man.

My hope for us in the pages ahead is that we will turn the gem and see how the light can refract differently this time. How might God, the Scriptures, the stories, and the trash we already know so well continue to teach us something new as we look at it from a different angle? Can we pull that trash can out from under the kitchen sink and take a second look at everything we so easily throw away? Are you ready to take a sacred journey into the unseen world of waste and find out what it means for the salvation of every person, every place, and every thing?

CHAPTER ONE

Beginning with the End

Nothing in all creation is hidden from God's sight. Everything is uncovered and laid bare before the eyes of him to whom we must give account.

Hebrews 4:13

Rev. Garbage-Man

Every summer seems more grueling than the last. Partially because it's hot and this old green GMC Sierra with a red door doesn't cool nor do the windows regularly roll down. Tennessee humidity is the worst. Today there is a pile stacked and thrown to the back of a house laying on the concrete. It's only 30 feet from the dumpster, but a pile this large isn't moved in a minute. This might be more than two truckloads worth of old remodel debris. It's made up of a pile of rotten wood, nails that I'm trying not to step on, insulation, and the worst part of almost any pile like this... plaster. You haven't hauled if you've never had to bag up and lift loads of plaster! I speedily begin the work of loading it in the back of the truck and pulling up next to the dumpster to toss it in. Walking it over would take all day, and I've learned that trucks are great tools. It still takes me a couple of hours. Bit by bit, the waste from this old house is thrown away, never to be seen again... at least not by me.

I am a trash hauler, even though the description on my business card reads, "Reconstruction and Recycling." If there is a house remodel, a new build, an eviction, or just a pile of junk in the yard, people call me to take it away. It's difficult, dirty work, the sort of work that keeps you humble. My hands in other people's trash, seeing everything society doesn't really want to see. Some call me the trash-man, but what most of my clients don't know is that I'm also an ordained minister.

People are usually pretty surprised when they find out that I'm not just the trash man, but also a member of the clergy. I've been pastoring for over ten years now and hauling garbage for about half that time. I never introduce myself as a pastor when I'm out working, so when someone discovers my *other* vocation, their entire demeanor often changes. When that information leaks out, you get the unique reaction that only occurs when you find out the guy who has been hauling your trash for years is also a reverend.

It is not unusual in the least for a pastor to be bi-vocational. I know many pastors who work in shoe shops and wait tables, but for whatever reason, the "garbage man" factor takes it to a new level for people. On the surface, we recognize these sorts of jobs as the leftovers, as the sort of jobs that people only do when they can't do anything else.

This profound but subtle sentiment lies at the heart of the issue of garbage. It is what has led to our current waste crisis in the world. That is the *unseen-ness* of waste. Garbage, especially in the west, is something that we want to remove from our sight. Even the people who must work with it are perhaps pitied for *what they have to do.* The issue is that we don't want to see, touch, or deal with our trash. Trash itself is thereby labeled as taboo or treated like a virus that needs to be contained. Waste is *someone else's* responsibility to deal with, not ours.

However, to begin the journey ahead of us we must see trash for what it is: ours. We must own it. Perhaps the first step to owning our waste has to do with getting a clearer picture of what is happening in the world.

A Garbage Emergency

In the fall of 2017, the beautiful Indonesian island of Bali declared a "garbage emergency."[1]

You might be thinking, *what in the world does that mean?*

Great question.

Ironically, Bali is one of those spots people talk about as being heaven on Earth, but the amount of trash washing up on their shores is changing that perception. Imagine going on a beach vacation with your family, but you have to share the ocean with old straws, plastic bags, bottles, and packaging. Monsoon season makes this a particularly difficult time for these places, as trash from all over the world can wash up on their shores.

If you travel from Bali to the other side of the Pacific Ocean, halfway between Hawaii and California lies what many have named the Great Pacific Garbage Patch. This area is estimated to cover 617,000 square miles, that's double the size of Texas, and it is full of floating trash! The Patch consists of chemical sludge, small microplastics, large fishing nets, and everything in between that has become trapped in the ocean's currents. [2] [3]

The problems aren't isolated to Bali and the Great Pacific Garbage Patch. Trash is everywhere and increasingly so, but you might only see it if you're willing to peer under the lid. The world produces over 2 billion tons of garbage every year. To haul away this much trash, we would need enough trucks to circle the world 24 times! America is truly a world leader. Leading world-wide trash production by producing over 382,000 tons of solid waste each day. America's solid waste alone would be equivalent to throwing away more than 14 full-size Statues of Liberty made of trash every single day, and America is just one country in a world full of trash producing societies. [4] [5]

Estimates show that if the world continues to develop at its current pace, trash will no longer be hidden behind the curtain but will be everywhere for us all to see. In many places around the world, garbage has already become the literal mountain in the room. One such example is in Lagos, Nigeria, where there is a struggle to maintain the balance between growth, development, and waste management as the population there has soared from 7 to 21 million residents in the past few decades. The result is trash piling up everywhere. The dump that was outside the city now finds itself nestled in the center of the action next to a local hospital and a neighboring school.

As we continue to grow and the world stretches to 8 billion people and beyond, more and more places will begin seeing the fate of Lagos. Lagos is a current micro-cosmic reflection of what is happening on the planet as a whole. All over the world, particularly in metropolitan areas, we will only continue to see the great iceberg of garbage arise as the camouflaging waters recede.

In Jakarta, the massively growing capital city of Indonesia, their rivers are quite literally flowing with trash. It has become so commonplace to deal with your trash by throwing it into their rivers, almost everyone does it. There is nowhere else for it to go!

In China, with over 1.4 billion citizens, their trash emergency is escalating. China collects over 230 million tons of household waste every year, and the piles are getting higher. In 2015, 73 people lost their lives in the Chinese city of Shenzhen from a landslide of garbage that had peaked, reaching over 500 feet into the air. The dumpsite, well over its capacity, gave-way claiming the lives of those there.[6]

Here in America, it doesn't feel so drastic because it seems as if we're keeping the problem "afloat." Meanwhile, every day in New York City, 3,600 tons of waste are put on barges and sent down the Hudson River. It is only a matter of time before our trash catches up to us. It is estimated that by 2030, we will need an entire second planet Earth to match our current rates of consumption of resources and the absorption of all our waste. This problem is beyond unsustainable. Here in the United States, we continue to ship our waste, truck it, and bury it anywhere we can.

Some developing countries can spend up to 50 percent of their budget on waste management.

The United States spends close to $200 billion a year on solid waste management and trash disposal.

Take a moment and allow that number to sink in.

That is estimated to be around the amount needed to end world hunger.

Obviously, we can't just pick up $200 billion from the federal government and give it to hungry people across the world, these figures and images ought to give us perspective. How could our posture change around our waste? How might we alter the decisions we are making in order to make the world better? How do we even go about getting a measurement on our own personal waste production? What can we even do to reduce waste in our own country and in the world?

The emergency of trash is even more difficult for city-dwellers, because unlike most utilities where we are charged for what we use, waste fees in metropolitan areas are often coming out as flat rates in our taxes. So, for most of us, these numbers are just not in front of us to see. They are more like all-you-can-eat buffets where you can load up your bins with as much as you can handle. Since we don't see how this problem is affecting our wallet, even usually-responsible Americans are just not really paying attention to the large amounts of waste we produce on a regular basis.

From our oceans to the overflowing bins in our metropolitan cul-de-sacs, there is hardly anywhere you can go in the world where you can't see a hint of our global garbage emergency.

Still, this issue seems extraordinarily difficult to care about. It's difficult to digest all this data and information. It seems so much simpler to shrug our shoulders and concede, "Someone, somewhere, is handling this." Should all this just remain out of sight, out of mind? Or could it be that we are incredibly overdue for a long hard look at our garbage? But where exactly are we looking? Because really, how much trash have you *seen* recently? [7] [8] [9]

Defining the Terms

Trash / Garbage
Everything that we throw away. This is everything in the disposal bin we are wheeling out to the street.

Waste
This term is being reserved for that which has no value. Waste means that something is not only discarded but is useless and seemingly unredeemable. (Although, by the end of this book, I hope you will come to see waste as a verb, not a noun.)

Recycle
To process our trash in such a way that makes it reusable.

Zero-Waste
Recycling or reusing all your trash in such a way that there is no waste left over.

Reclaim
To take something old and used and repurpose it for something new.

Compost
Decayed organic material that becomes fertilizer.

Landfill
A place where the trash we throw away is piled up and buried in the Earth.

The Illusion

Have you seen your garbage lately?

Week by week, we roll our garbage cans to the street. They are full of household waste, food scraps, old packaging, and really, whatever we want. It sort of feels like magic. You can pretty much put anything you want in that can and wheel it to the street, and it disappears.

Magic, right?

It isn't really magic, but it is an illusion.

At some point during the day, usually when you're not looking, a couple of people roll up in their garbage truck, hook up your can, empty it out, and your garbage rolls away to land-fill-land. In other words, what's happening is you are relocating your waste. It's simply being moved away from *your* land to land somewhere else. As it happens, this trash trick isn't very magical after all.

For years, I've gotten into a truck every day to drive around Nashville and haul off all sorts of stuff: remodel debris, rotten moldy furniture, practically brand-new appliances, metal pots and pans, yards full of belongings from families just evicted, clothes, kitchens full of leftover , closets full of forgotten photos, more wood than you can shake a stick at (pun intended), pallets, drywall, plastic bottles for days, and on and on. If I could somehow pile up everything that I've personally hauled off over the years, it would take over an entire neighborhood.

Waste.

Trash.

Junk.

That's a lot of stuff. That's a lot of material. That's a lot of waste, and that's just one dude in one truck, hauling junk. So it's a pretty big deal that I recycle, reuse, and repurpose everything that I possibly can! Yet even then, the amount of trash is still overwhelming.

Not that long ago, I talked with a group of students about recycling and waste, and I challenged them to name something that was 100% total waste. As in, what is something that has no value left, no repurposing or recycling qualities about it? What is something that is without a doubt unredeemable garbage? So, they started naming some typical trash items...

"Banana peels."

"Nope, compost," I'd say.

"Kroger bags!"

"No, recyclable."

"Old TVs"

"No, recyclable as electronics."

"An old car."

"No, that's metal... recyclable."

"Poop!" (inevitable high school banter)

"Nope, definitely compostable!"

Now of course, there are items that are actually waste and can't be used for anything anymore. This conversation is not as black and white as my challenge to these unsuspecting high school students. The point is, that most of the stuff we think is waste, is in fact not. It's not that most waste can't be reused or recycled, it's that many of us were never taught a posture of responsibility or given the know-how to properly manage our waste. To be fair, our trash is hidden away leaving many of us unaware of what's taking place behind the trash-scenes of our day.

I grew up in the country hills of Tennessee – rural southern America y'all. On our dirt road, there was no service taking off our trash in clone-like, suburb-style bins. No garbage truck ever drove there, and there were definitely no recycling trucks! We had a recycling and waste convenience center about a ten-minute drive away, and whenever we had a sufficient enough pile of trash stacked up in the garage, we'd haul it off. Or, if the smell got bad enough, you knew it was time! I grew up in a place and time that if there were large items to be thrown away, you might just see someone rolling them off a hill or burying them with their tractor! Recycling was just not a big part of our culture and not just because of the inconvenience of it.

From a young age, I was taught about gardening and caring for the Earth. A close relationship with plants and animals came second nature for me. Yet these lessons never correlated much to the products that were inside our home. Nor did I ever draw the connection from caring for the soil to what was in our kitchen wastebasket... and certainly, I hadn't understood trash in the context of my relationship with God! This all would come much later.

Today, at my home in metropolitan Nashville, we have two street recycle bins and one trash bin. At our worst, we will roll out all three once a month. But even then, our trash bin just isn't that full after three or four weeks. Our trash becomes a little less every year now, as we are discovering new ways to recycle, reduce, and repurpose. Since moving to the city, I've felt a little spoiled in the recycling department. Not everyone has the luxury of curbside recycling. Not having a system to do part of the work for you requires much more intentionality.

This work of dealing with waste is a journey that we are still on today in our home and every home and business across the world, whether rural or urban. Because, well, it's *our* trash, isn't it? If it is, where should we put it? What should we do with it?

It's often entertaining to watch the vigor in which some folks throw things away! I sometimes wonder if actual endorphins are kicking in when we chuck large amounts of stuff into a dumpster! There's a noticeable tinge of joy as people get the chance to smash something old on its way out. This is probably due to our society's lack of primal activities (An amusing example of this is the current surge in ax throwing places in our city!). Part of my job often involves having to destroy old rotten furniture, so it fits into the truck. I typically give this task to any younger help I might have for the day, because as they always tell me, "This is so fun!"

Maybe a better example is when someone takes out a huge bag of trash they've collected in their house and leave behind a bit cleaner looking home. It's a great feeling to have accomplished something and gained a tidier living space, but this is part of the issue. We are just moving our unwanted items from our space to another space. We're not necessarily getting rid of these items but relocating them. It all goes somewhere, and that somewhere is a place we should be thinking about. Every piece of old furniture or household trash that leaves our home must *always* find a new home. This new home will *always* be somewhere on our common home we call planet Earth.

Every day, somewhere likely not too far from where you live, a large truck backs up to an ever-increasing mountain of waste and unloads its haul. There's a bit of mourning that should happen as we cover these disposed of scraps with dirt to be buried in the growing cemetery of stuff. These funerals are endlessly taking place as you and I continue to attempt to grapple with the surmounting issue of a culture of wastefulness. These mounds or dumps, as we like to call them, can reach over 1,000 feet above sea level and cover as much as 700 acres of land. Currently, there are over 2,000 landfills spread across the United States. The more we continue to grow these large peaks of waste, future generations will be the ones continuing to deal with toxins, greenhouse gases, and other likely issues currently unforeseen. [1] [2]

Landfills are a horrendous stew full of everything you can imagine. Even so much of what isn't supposed to end up in these sites are constantly thrown in - things like batteries, lightbulbs, chemicals, and oil. These items should never just be tossed in with the kitchen trash because they are hazardous materials. Yet, I see it all the time. These mounds become full of chemicals, toxins, harmful gasses, and other dangerous additives that are harmful to us and our planet. Depending on your recycling convenience center, there just isn't anyone there "policing" your waste or sorting through your bag of kitchen trash. It's just all finding its way into that ever-growing Kilimanjaro of trash.

Americans throw away about 4.4lbs of stuff on average every day. That's about double the global average. Of that, only 1.5lbs is separated to be recycled or composted, leaving 2.9lbs going in the trash bin. This may not sound like a lot, but it is. Nationally, this becomes a yearly total of 139,600,000 tons making its way to our landfills. It is estimated that at least half of this number, could be recycled, composted, or salvaged if we were simply more intentional about it! This would be like throwing away something the size of the Golden Gate Bridge, 85 times over! This is how much unrecycled but recyclable material Americans waste in a year. [3] [4]

In the U.S., our landfills are still hit annually with:

30.63 million tons of food

26.82 million tons of plastic

18.35 million tons of paper and paperboard

13.8 million tons of metals

12.14 million tons of wood

11.15 million tons of textiles

8.65 million tons of yard trimmings

6.87 million tons of glass[5]

With simply a glance at this list, it's not difficult to see how much of this should be recycled, composted, or reclaimed. Just packaging itself takes up a bulk of this landfill pie. Think for a moment about every box, bag, or container your food comes in, or the packages that are delivered to your doorstep in a year's time. In 2019, Amazon delivered 3.5 billion packages worldwide. That's over 9,000,000 packages delivered per day, and that's just Amazon! That's a lot of cardboard and a multitude of bubble-wrap that must go somewhere (Not to mention the products inside!). [6]

But at the end of the day, these issues of ever-increasing wastefulness aren't solved by digging larger craters in the ground or even simply becoming better recyclers (Although we all must!). No, we must now peel another layer off the top. We must walk further upstream.[7] We must ask the next question begging to be asked: Why are so many things being thrown away and what sort of creature lurks behind such wastefulness of creation?

Landfills of Deception

"Who is like the beast, and who can fight against it?"
- Revelation 13:4

What's striking about working in the "garbage business" is that you witness everything under the sun being thrown away. I've seen things tossed in dumpsters that Oscar the Grouch would gawk at! Frequently the calls we get for trash

hauling are simply homes of belongings that have been aban-
doned or left unwanted. This happens in *both* the wealthy
and poverty-stricken parts of town. In fact, we owe much of
what we "own" around our home today from hauling! From
our Sleep Number bed to our coffee maker, somebody at
some point, called us to haul it away.

Whenever I share stories about trash hauling and all the
things I've had to get rid of, I'm always asked, "Why do people
leave all this stuff behind?" Unfortunately, the answers are
never as clear cut as the questions. Some people just move
and don't care about taking things they have been wanting to
get rid of. Others just can't afford moving services, so they
pile in what fits in the car in the time frame they have. Some
people are wealthy and want a fresh start with new stuff. And
there are dozens of other reasons in between those of why
things get left behind at a property.

One of the more unfortunate sites trash haulers witness regularly is evictions. For those of you unfamiliar, a landlord will
start the eviction process when someone doesn't pay their
rent for a certain amount of time. If this happened to you, you
would get served an eviction notice by a law enforcement of-
ficer explaining the eviction and the date by which you must
be out of your house or apartment. On the specified date, law
enforcement visits you again, though hopefully, you have already left the property. This time, they come into your home
and grab everything they can in a short amount of time and
throw it onto the front lawn. Usually, by the time this

happens, the tenants have left and taken what is most valuable to them. Often, tenants take whichever of their precious belongings they can fit into their car, and anything that doesn't fit gets left behind. Seeing an entire home poured out into the front yard like a giant toy-bin shaken and turned upside down, is a sad and sobering sight. It produces the scene you would picture if a big box store, a dollar store, and an infomercial got together one night and threw a crazy party. And wouldn't you know, I usually get an invitation to come the next morning for the cleanup party.

Observing these belonging "grave-yards" has often caused me to reflect on just how many things we possess. This stuff-abundance is a wealthy person's issue just as much as it is for those of more meager households. Together as a culture, we seem to have reached a new threshold of possessing more than ever before.

Every corner of our homes and lives is filled with textiles, trinkets, and toys. Why is this? Part of the answer is that we have an overabundance of materiality. There is just more stuff than we know what to do with!

Occasionally, I find myself walking into a Costco, and when that blast of air splashes my hair, I briefly lose my breath gazing in awe at the monstrosity of our aisles of never-ending supply and demand. In your everyday comings and goings, you may not notice this abundance. Just as the frog doesn't know he's in boiling water until it's too late. But every house, office, store-front, school, and back-alley are jam-packed with their own "belongings." There is simply a multitude of possessions in the world today. Since the turn of the century and the age of the industrial revolution, we have been producing new material at amazing capacities, and we're only getting quicker at it. Factories work around the clock to meet consumer wants and desires. After over 100 years of this, we've accumulated quite a collection of "goods" as a society... if we can call it that.

"Goods" is a questionable term for these items.

Along with an overabundance, another crucial factor in our planet-of-stuff is an item's value. The "cheapness" of goods today creates immense problems for our lives and our planet, under the guise of helping us live better. We have a mass collection of disposable belongings, and there, we easily become sucked into the hells of cheap living. Much of what's produced today isn't made from hard or durable raw material as it was hundreds of years ago. Ironically, with all the progress we've made as a society we now produce things more low-quality than generations before us. We have the ability to produce higher-quality goods than ever before in history. Yet, instead of leveraging our technology for consumer gain, corporations have leveraged it for stockholder gain. Low-quality plastic cogs and wheels inside my tools and devices will give it just a short enough lifespan for me to need another one in a couple of years or less.

We know this as a society: so much of what we purchase for our homes and everyday lives just isn't high quality. Yet somehow, we've been ok with this. I'm sure that you have experienced this at some point with something you've purchased. The phrase, "They just don't make 'em like they used to," was a mantra I heard growing up. Although, it's not all our fault. Finding quality products hasn't been the easiest task, especially over the last few decades (unless you're purchasing your goods from the Amish). So, it's not that big of a surprise when people couldn't care less what they throw away because it feels that many of their belongings just aren't high quality enough.

We live as if this is just the way it is and has to be. Meanwhile, marketing and commercials twist words and shine lights to make you believe you're buying a product of amazing quality for an unheard-of low price. But rolling back prices doesn't leave everyone with smiling faces. Of course, there is a secret reason why these items are so affordable: the quantity. The cheapness and the deception have left us in an active and living landfill. Everything in your possession is on its way to be eaten by this great beast dressed in sheep's clothing. It is disguised as "betterment," but its teeth are deadly. The catch is, unbeknownst to us, this beast we've created may even consume its makers.

A couple of years ago we had our appliance repair person out. The "new" used washer we had bought was leaking again. On the outset, it was the fanciest appliance we'd ever owned. It had so many buttons and whistles that you wanted to drive it around the block with sunglasses on! But the shimmer and shine turned out to be a façade as it continued to also wash our laundry room floor. Half-way through a major washer open-heart-surgery, the repairman, with his hands covered in grease, just looked at me and shook his head. At that point, I knew it was over.

What was the deal? Why couldn't we just fix it? Could it really be that bad?

As I engaged in conversation with this friendly repairman who literally made his living repairing appliances, he tells me that almost every appliance he sees that's been made in the last several years, "Just isn't any good."

Just isn't any good. What is that supposed to mean?

How is this possible? What are we supposed to do? Where are we supposed to shop? Should we buy a washboard and basin?

We engage in a lengthy conversation around washer brands and the appliance industry, in which the clearest consensus was somehow, "You know, the older ones are just the best ones."

Really? The older ones are the best ones? I should just go out to the scrapyard and find a fixer-upper? What's our home-owner protocol here?

Somehow, as technology continues to progress to a level never seen before, a new washing machine still only lasts about 5 years. There is something sinister happening below the surface.

Down in the subterranean sewers, flowing underneath this entire highway of cheapness, is a world of garbage by design. This is called "designed for the dump" or "planned obsolescence." These are items that are manufactured with a short lifespan in mind. Therefore, not only is there a lack of durability in so many products today, but also an actual predisposition for a timely decay. Designed obsolescence is a sobering reality that exists behind the appliances, toys, and technologies we buy. I'm positive you've experienced this with some appliance or electronic you've purchased in the last few years.

Large corporations realized that if they make these household items and electronics too well, and they last too long, they won't sell as much. Obviously. With planned obsolescence, you'll have to go get a new TV in a few years and another hairdryer just in time for Christmas. This puts the consumer in a difficult spot. Because there doesn't appear to be that many trustworthy companies that are creating real hardy products that have long lifespans. But also, even if there are better options, it's typically only the upper class who can afford them. So, how might we begin to change all this? Are we, as a society, doomed to the devouring beast of greedy progress and its paws of planned obsolescence? [8] [9] [10]

Waste-Woke

Something is fascinating about home remodel shows. It's mesmerizing to see a space transformed from outdated to modern. There is something beautiful about cutting, shaping, crafting, and painting new material into a usable new home environment.

Yet, what happens to the old house? What about that wall the sledgehammer so thrillingly gets smashed in with? What happens to all of that material? Often, we have said with our actions that outdated material has little to no value so you might as well have fun destroying it before throwing it away. This is an honest and typically innocent sentiment.

We live in an age when we've been mostly focused on the question, "Can we do it?" rather than, "Should we do it?" The only measuring rod we've used is if our pocketbooks can bear the weight of such an upgrade.

Have you ever stopped in front of the garbage can for a moment and wondered about the intrinsic value of what you're getting rid of?

Do you know the value of your trash?

Have you ever considered material to have an inherent value?

Have you ever thought about it having worth beyond its usefulness for your project, your home, or your life?

Does this material in our possession have value outside of us "giving" value to it?

This line of questioning may sound a little "out there" to you, but just hang with me. What if this old house actually possesses value because it is also part of God's good creation, and not simply because it is useful for you and me?

Many people out there are aware of and care about the "afterlife" of their possessions. At the end of the day, I don't think anyone intentionally wants anything to go to waste. A lot of us, myself included, in an effort to do our part and feel better about our progress, often hope and rely on places such as Habitat for Humanity's ReStore. We take our expired belongings to thrift stores, like the ReStore, in hopes of it finding a future home. Sometimes this does happen, and donating is without a doubt, a good thing to do.

Yet, the unforeseen consequences lurk as we make subtle justifications for our household expansions. Places like Goodwill help us feel better about our new purchases and keeping up with the Joneses. The truth is places like Habitat's ReStore and Goodwill are often overwhelmed and inundated with an overabundance of stuff. We like to think the scraps from our table are feeding someone else, but this is frequently untrue. Multiple times, I've pulled up to the ReStore with a truck full of sinks and cabinets to donate, and they had so much that they couldn't receive my donation.

Thousands of donations and clothing items from Goodwill never sell and simply end up being shipped overseas to the developing world, wreaking havoc on their economies and land. In the end, much of our clothing and material just ends up in landfills in someone else's community or backyard. What's worse is that a great deal of these "landfill donations" don't break down or decompose as one might think. Sadly, these items are lying in the Earth for hundreds of years, often releasing toxins into the soil and greenhouse gas into the atmosphere. [11] [12]

It is not that you should never make donations, but we should all be asking questions about the fate of our donations. What are the chances someone is going to buy this second-hand? Is there a better way to ensure this item's life can be extended? Are there better places to donate than others who are more responsible with their waste?

We should also take this line of questioning right back to the checkout line and start asking ourselves some questions before we purchase anything new. Questions like: How long will I use this item? What do I plan to do with it when I can't use it anymore? Or better yet, can I buy this item used, so that I'm not contributing to an increased demand for new products from raw materials? How might we begin answering the question of waste from the very beginning of our relationship with each and every item?

At the beginning, we must confront the end.

If I buy this, what will become of it in a month? In a year? In 10 years?

Can I repurpose it beyond its foreseeable lifespan? Is it recyclable? Is it biodegradable?

How long will this last? Can this be repaired if broken?

These questions must become our criteria for "progress." We must measure success not by how much we are consuming, but how we are saving. We must reframe what is most important.

To make this explicitly clear, our first questions must not be:

Can I make money from this? How lucrative is this?

Is this a good deal? Is this on sale?

Does this purchase make me feel good?

This is the wrong starting place. We must begin with the end in mind.

Taking care of and being a good steward of our belongings is a virtue as old as Little House on the Prairie, except back in those days, your goods really mattered. Back then, if your lantern or hand saw broke, you were going to be in a tough spot. For thousands of years, there was no cruising down to the superstore or ordering a replacement online. Fast forward into the future and today, we stand on the edge of critical decisions as consumers and producers. Will we continue to be good stewards in a virtuous relationship with our material goods? Taking care of the Earth can feel a little less about virtue and a lot less personal today as our trash wheels away into the unknown, but in order to continue being good stewards of creation in our own time, we must be willing to alter our habits of consumption like never before in human history.

This may sound absurd and daunting, but we certainly hold the keys to dismantling that which we ourselves have constructed. The future could be a win-win for everyone if we are willing to take a stand as consumers and bend as producers. We currently have the option to create a more heaven-like tomorrow or to march on with the type of "progress" that leads to finding ourselves in the landfills of hell.

If our demeanor towards the material that we possess is always expendable, "Buy One, Get One," or "If it breaks, I'll buy another," then the personal value we place on these objects diminishes more and more and more. This will continue to happen until we care so little for our possessions that we treat them like trash from day one.

What if we were never meant to objectify any object?

What if we're called to care for every possession in our possession?

How might we treat every belonging like it *belongs?*

In the chapters ahead I will invite you to become "waste-woke." So open your minds, open your Bibles, open your receptacles, and let's take a look.

Respond & Reflect

Respond

→ *Keep all your own waste.*

Just for a few days pretend that there is no such thing as a landfill or a bin that you can wheel out to the street. Take those trash cans and put them away. Every item that you were going to throw away or get rid of, do your best to repurpose, recycle, or compost! Try to carry some of your trash around with you for just one week. Keep it in your home. Keep it in your car. Keep it in your backpack. Keep it in your pockets. Keep it in your purse.

By doing this, you will quickly see just how much one person consumes and just how much waste one person can produce in a short period. Most of us do not have a garbage perspective.

After 3 days, attempt to lay out all of the trash you have produced and take a photo. Then bag it up and place it on a scale. You can post this photo online with #GarbageTheologyBook to see how you compare with others!

Try it – just one week! If you want to stretch yourself, try it for a month!

Reflect

What does this challenge stir within you?

If the moment after you finish with an item, it goes into the trash bin, you have likely lived your entire life disillusioned about the amount of waste you produce.

In doing this practice, what have you noticed, not just about your waste habits but also about your consumption habits?

Was there a particular statistic that stood out to you in this chapter?

How have you experienced the smothering presence of an overabundance of stuff in your life?

Where have you seen planned obsolescence before? Why do you think this exists?

Does this chapter challenge the way you think about garbage? In what way?

What are some things we must change to begin fixing this "trash emergency?"

What do you think any of this has to do with your faith?

→ Visit www.storyofstuff.org to learn more about where our "stuff" comes from.

CHAPTER TWO

Divine Recycler

On December 7th, 1972, the crew of the Apollo 17 spacecraft, on their way to the moon, peered back at the Earth and snapped the famous image known as The Blue Marble.[1] From 18,000 miles away this photograph has inspired thousands to contemplate more deeply on our unique placement in the Universe. All life as we know it has only and always existed on this blue sphere we call home. From space, it becomes clear that no boundaries or lines are dividing this country from that one. Looking back at the Earth, we see that we are one people, part of this one environment, on this one planet. Together. Inseparable.

Unfortunately, many of us have come to understand ourselves as separate beings from the world in which we live. As if there is humanity, and then there is the Earth that we live on. Yet we are not a people on a planet, we are a people of a planet. We are all indigenous to this home we call planet Earth.

Some folks argue that God takes care of us, and so we shouldn't be that concerned if our planet is being harmed. God does take care of us; yet what if the way God continually does this is through our relationship with one another and with the Earth?

If we believe God is the Creator then we will surely see the divine plan of how we are strategically placed inside an ecosystem, on a planet, and as a part of a creation.

Our lives are inseparably intertwined with the Earth.

We are Earthlings, made into the image of our Creator.

But what is our creator like?

The Salvaging God

Consider your own call, brothers and sisters: not many of you were wise by human standards, not many were powerful, not many were of noble birth. But God chose what is foolish in the world to shame the wise; God chose what is weak in the world to shame the strong; God chose what is low and despised in the world, things that are not, to reduce to nothing things that are, so that no one might boast in the presence of God. He is the source of your life in Christ Jesus, who became for us wisdom from God, and righteousness and sanctification and redemption, in order that, as it is written, "Let the one who boasts, boast in the Lord."
- **1 Corinthians 1:26-31**

Nobody likes waste.

I'm convinced there is something inside us all that rejects the idea of waste, but I suppose like anything that we do day in and day out, you get used to it.

This is something that I have recognized and love about my oldest daughter, Story. Story does not "do" waste. If you want to throw away some packaging or scrap containers while she is in the room, you'll need to hide doing it! Even before we can toss the empty toilet paper roll into the recycling bin, she grabs it and declares, "Don't throw that away. I need that for my art!" That girl is all over reusing and repurposing things around her. Our living room and the kitchen are often decorated with scraps of trash made into guitars, oatmeal containers decorated for storing jewelry, or just a giant box that is now a permanent playhouse next to the refrigerator. She is scrappy, she is prolific, and she is most definitely not wasteful. But the most fascinating part of it all is that this isn't something that we drill into her. These notions of intrinsic value for even our trash are something she came pre-programmed with. Her first question has always been, "Why are you throwing that away?" not, "Why are you keeping that?"

Odds are when you were a child you did some of this, too. I know when I was a kid I would explore and glean the fields of my grandfather's workbench and collect the dregs of my dad's shop. I have distinct memories of nailing old tires onto our nice outdoor playhouse that my dad had built because, well, it needed windows, right? Over time, I would add some old rope here and some grungy car parts there. Later in my 20's, I was very upset when I discovered my dad had torn the playhouse down! Looking back, I suppose it did appear to be a building code violation meets *Sanford and Sons*.

What is it exactly that makes us instinctual salvagers at a young age before anyone teaches us about "throwing things away"?

As we get older, a remnant of that remains, doesn't it? When something gets wasted, it feels as if we've lost the game. If you've ever spent tons of time on a project just to see it fail; if you've ever poured money, energy, and resources into a business or a new idea just to see the whole thing fall apart; if you've ever invested heavily only to lose money on a venture, then you know what I'm talking about. You've felt that feeling before, haven't you?

It is an unmistakable aversion toward waste.

This idea that you will not get back all the work, funds, assets, sweat, and blood that you put into a thing begs the question, "What was it all for?" It can be haunting because inside all of us is something that doesn't jive with waste. It's just not something we are wired to enjoy. In fact, it's quite the opposite! When life feels streamlined and productive, when nothing is getting wasted and everything is meeting its potential, that's when we are really grooving. You know that feeling. It's like you're going through your day high fiving the universe! That meeting was a success! The kids ate all their dinner! You made great progress on that project! It's the type of day that you just throw on some Stevie Wonder and roll on.

But there are those other days, too. The days that seem to bother us the most are the ones when it feels as if everything is unproductive, slow, and un-accomplished. When it just seems nothing is moving forward.

The point is, the concept of waste goes against the very core of our creative being. When you are created in the image of a Creator, you will be a creator at your core, and no creator wants to see his or her creation going to waste.

Because waste... well, that feels like failure.

Waste is loss.

Waste is what happens when things have gone wrong.

Waste is what happens when the recipe is off.

Waste isn't simply about inefficiency, but about being outside of what you were made for.

You spent all those years in that venture, giving yourself to that company, birthing this new business, and the thought we hate the most is that it would all go to waste. It's no new idea that wastefulness at its root seems to swim against the very flow of our being.

What I find most interesting in the arc of the Biblical narrative is how God, over and over, uses the people that are least successful in society to be God's hands and feet. God always chooses those who are weak, barren, outcast, thrown into a pit, slow to speak, too old, the wrong gender, and slaves to the system to be the ones to carry the good news forward. The very story of the people of God is a story about an "unsuccessful" group of people called to be God's means of blessing to the world.

We see it way back in Genesis 12 with God's call to the landless Abram and barren Sarai. To the two people in that time who would be considered lacking in their culture due to their being landless and barren. God promises, "I will make of you a great nation, and I will bless you, and make your name great, so that you will be a blessing."

This is one of the things that makes the narrative of the kingdom of God so captivating. Our Creator stubbornly insists on choosing the people whom society would deem a "waste" to do God's work in the world. It is precisely these sorts of folk that God sends to be our leaders and teachers. From Abraham and Sarah to Joseph who was sold into slavery by his brothers, to the harlot Rahab in Jericho, and the wild prophet Elijah, God deliberately chooses the things that represent the least in the world to deliver God's greatest messages. Our God is a God who loves to collect from the recycling bin and scavenge through our pile of not-good-enoughs to find exactly what is needed.

If you need further proof, look into the stories of Esther, Simeon, Onesimus, and the mixed bag of fishers and tax-collector disciples Jesus chooses.

Our God has always been more interested in salvaging creation rather than discarding and upgrading!

God has always been about repurposing rather than tossing.

Renewing rather than getting rid of.

Recycling rather than trashing.

Resurrecting rather than eradicating.

Truly our God is a salvaging God.

I wonder what else Scripture might have to say about our Creator God's character.

Pure Goodness

Where were you when I laid the foundation of the Earth?
　Tell me, if you have understanding.
Who determined its measurements—surely you know!
　Or who stretched the line upon it?
On what were its bases sunk,

or who laid its cornerstone
when the morning stars sang together
  and all the heavenly beings shouted for joy?
– **Job 38:4-7**

I love to think about God as the Creator at the beginning of all things. I just imagine God there with an empty canvas ready to burst forth light and love all over the blank page of eternity! We cannot fathom such love, such intentionality, such precision, such creative juices that must have been flying from the holy fingertips of God. It's no secret that our Genesis poem has captivated our imaginations for thousands of years.

Imagine with me...

In the beginning, God created the heavens and the Earth; the Earth was a formless void and darkness covered the face of the deep, while a wind from God swept over the face of the waters.

God takes six beautiful days to create the light and separate the light from the darkness, to create water and sky, land and vegetation, sun, moon and stars, sea creatures and birds of the air, animals to crawl upon the Earth, and at last, humanity.

And then, finally, on the seventh day after all this creating... God throws away the packaging!

Wait, what!?

No, despite popular beliefs, God did not order the heavens and the Earth from Amazon! It's a funny anecdote, but it does call to attention something very striking about the way God creates. It reminds us that when God creates - it is pure. There is no packaging. There are no cardboard boxes to toss at the end. There is no bubble wrap thrown to the side. There are no packing peanuts scattered all over God's living room floor.

When God creates, there is no excess.

There are no scraps left over.

There are no bins to toss the "oops" bit of creation in!

There's only pure unadulterated creation.

In Genesis, God creates, and it says, "God saw that it was good." *Tov* is the word in Hebrew that we typically translate as "good." Although, at its core, *tov* means "appropriate." When God calls his creation *tov*, it's more than just saying "that will do" or "it's good" (versus it being bad). God calls his creation *tov* because it is perfectly created and incarnated to do the very thing it is formed to do. It has everything it needs to be what it is here for. It is wholly appropriate.

God calling creation *tov* means that every bit of creation is not only intentional in its design, but it is also an essential part of the whole web of life that is the creation, the Earth, the ecosystem, and the universe. Our creation narrative is the first hint we have of just how elaborate God's creative ways are. We are interwoven with all of creation into this beautifully interconnected and intentional divine narrative.

You cannot deny the magnificent and flawless interplay that happens in all of nature. It's something that I'm convinced we are still in our infancy of understanding, the interwoven miracles that exist right under our fingernails and tucked underneath the soil! From the largest mysteries to the smallest, we can see just how truly amazing it is when we consider that we aren't any closer to understanding the depths of microbial life as we are to comprehending the expanse of the stars!

We are just now discovering the surprising "purposes" of plants or wildlife that might have previously appeared troublesome! Think about stinging nettle for instance. If you touch this plant, it might cause lots of irritation, redness, and itching. Yet, ironically, this plant also contains many potential healing and pain-relieving properties. It is most commonly known for use against arthritis and against seasonal allergies! Also, many gardeners grow this in their gardens because it acts as a great fertilizer aid. Or consider purple deadnettle with its small blossoms which are typically thought of as a weed in our yard. It can be used as an anti-inflammatory, good for reducing allergy symptoms, edible, and nutritious!

The more we know we should be living in sync with nature, the more we can grow as societies in the world. One innovative discovery that taps into creation's interconnected and appropriate connection is currently happening on an algae farm in Hawaii. The company called Global Algae Innovations is growing and extracting oil from algae and creating refined fuel from it! They are making clean biofuel that can function just like gasoline or even jet fuel from a seemingly unwanted plant. Not only that, on just a handful of acres, they are able to produce more hearty protein from algae for feeding farm animals than other industrial-sized farms are able to produce elsewhere with common methods. Thus, instead of fracking for crude oil, which is dangerous to humans and pollutes the environment, this company has found a way forward that benefits all parties involved. Unless our innovations are good news for all of creation, I'm not sure we can call it good news. Companies like Global Algae Innovations are changing the world as they're probing into the natural gifts of creation. [2]

If our progress is constantly harming our planet and leaving mounds of toxic waste behind, then we are not creating in the footsteps of our own Creator.

What if waste was never part of God's good plan? What if living into the image of God involves redeeming the things around us which society has called trash? What if our calling as the people of God on Earth always involves the resurrection of those things deemed worthless? What if the more we draw close to our Creator, the less excess there can be in our own lives and in our own creations?

What if the further we reflect the image of our Creator God, the further we disclose the beauty and holy wholeness of creation? What if we are simply at the early stages of understanding the planet and how appropriately we can live? And what if living into our God-given creative destiny isn't connected with how many resources we are consuming, but has more to do with how much creative potential we are unlocking?

What if the more we discern the *tov* of God's created order, the more our lives will make sense?

What if, as we grew to understand creation, we discovered that there are no foes, only misunderstood friends! Just maybe, we live on a planet full of *tov*!

From Creation, For Creation

Then God said, "Let the Earth bring forth grass, the herb that yields seed, and the fruit tree that yields fruit according to its kind, whose seed is in itself, on the Earth"; and it was so.
– **Genesis 1:11**

I love talking about Genesis if you haven't noticed, yet. This ancient narrative has so much meaning for us today. I'm convinced that the more we understand these primal stories and the deep truths they are conveying for human history, the more you and I will find ourselves at peace with God, ourselves, and the Earth. Embracing what these ancient words have to teach us aid in reconnecting the dots between ourselves, all of humanity, every other bit of creation, and materiality. So, let's briefly jump into the second chapter of Genesis which is commonly referred to as the "second creation story" or the "zoomed-in version" of the narrative. At verse 4 it begins:

This is the detailed story of the Eternal God's singular work in creating all that exists. On the day the heavens and Earth were created, there were no plants or vegetation to cover the Earth. The fields were barren and empty, because the Eternal God had not sent the rains to nourish the soil or anyone to tend it. In those days, a mist rose up from the ground to blanket the Earth, and its vapors irrigated the land. One day the Eternal God scooped dirt out of the ground, sculpted it into the shape we call human, breathed the breath that gives life into the nostrils of the human, and the human became a living soul.[3]

These verses are so rich with meaning for us today. It says, there were no herbs or plants springing up because first, it had not rained, and second, there were no humans to serve the ground.

Isn't this fascinating, that in the very beginning there is this symbiotic relationship between us and the Earth? We most assuredly need the Earth and its many gifts to live. There is no doubt that nature has an agency all to itself to be healing and life-giving. Yet, let us consider, might the Earth thrive even more if we were here serving and protecting it? Might the ground in fact flourish under the care of humanity's hands? It's not hard today to think about how the planet would be doing much better off without us... but imagine for a moment, if humanity were to live here on Earth as we were originally created to do. Could the Earth *prosper* with our care?

This is certainly something to germinate on (pun intended)!

Perhaps, it now gets even more interesting. God created us *out of* the ground. The Hebrew term here is often just translated as "man," but the term is *ha adam* meaning "the human." The word for "ground" is *adamah.* If you were reading Hebrew, you would not be able to miss the connection; God creates the *ha adam* out of the *adamah.* Literally translated, humanity is birthed right out of the ground, given life with the breath of God! We are humans from humus!

Why is this so significant?

You and I are made from the same material as the rest of creation. We are literally of the Earth. We are Earthlings. We are pulled from the ground and brought to life by the breath of God entering our bodies. We are lumps of dirt created in the image of God, a miracle in and of itself.

You and I cannot be separated from the ground beneath our feet. We are one. Created from it and here to serve it as it serves us. This symbiotic relationship was ordained from the start. We are not a people separate from the Earth, as if we live on top of it, grazing it for our needs until we need it no longer. But we are tethered with the Earth, along with everything that comes from the Earth.

We are descendants of the Adam and the atom. Now we can look into a microscope and see the great atomic world that connects us all to everything. It's why they say we are made of stars! This atomic matter that you and I and the entire universe consist of never goes away. It remains. You can throw it in a landfill; it can decay in a grave; it can shoot off and disintegrate into the sun. But matter remains. It just forms into a different, new life than before.

Look around you. Everything you see has also sprung up from this *adamah*, every piece of furniture and appliance, every article of clothing and patch of carpet. We are surrounded by ourselves, by this common ground. Genesis and science have even been syncing up on this idea for many years now.

Sound familiar? It is no coincidence that the narrative of loss and renewal is weaved into the very fabric of the universe, and that Christ came and modeled this exact pattern for us all to follow and embrace. We are holy adamah. Set apart, given breath by the Spirit of God, so that in the image of God, we might also create, serve, and protect creation. Not discard it.

Centuries ago the infamous astrologer, Galileo, endured persecution as he unmasked the inaccuracy of the wide-held belief that the sun revolves around us! Of course, we now know that the Earth revolves around the Sun. But I can't help but think that, similarly today, we often falsely believe that the natural world revolves around us. As if the Earth exists solely for your well-being. But the Earth doesn't revolve around us. We are born of the Earth, not the other way around. The more we treat our home as a single-use product whose only purpose is for our momentary drink, we will inevitably leave nothing behind for future generations. In the end, we won't be able to order a new planet when this one is too polluted and disregarded to provide for us anymore.

The Earth is deteriorating because of our harmful assumptions. The moment that we place ourselves at the center of the world rather than as the servant of the world, we find that we're still missing the whole thing. But our roots confirm that our story has never been anthropocentric. We are together with all creation, reflecting back the glory and image of our Great Creator. God is the center, not us. Our propensity to put ourselves at the center of the universe has been our short-sighted, shortcoming for ages.

If you can believe it, this Genesis narrative gets even juicier! By verse 15, we learn that God has placed humanity in the garden to work it and keep it. Again, many translations will say "till and keep" but the term here is *avad,* which in the Old Testament frequently means "serve." God's purpose for us here doesn't get much clearer than Genesis 2:15. We are here to serve and protect (or keep) this garden we call home.

Again, isn't this so backward from how it seems our relationship with the Earth is today in much of the western world? We are so convinced that this garden is at our disposal! We are so sure everything exists here for our consumption and benefit. Our self-centered posture has been our great sin since we first took a bite of that forbidden fruit. It is the sinful "consumption assumption."

Yet, how amazing to think that this relationship might be flipped on its head! You and I are given the opportunity to breathe life into this planet just as God breathed life into each of us.

How might you reach down, take a piece of *adamah*, and breathe life into it? How might you reorient your relationship with your every possession? How might you think about your work here on Earth being transformed by living into this sacred relationship?

As this zoomed-in origin narrative comes to a close, we see the multiplicity of God's creation at work. Our God multiplies and calls us to do the same. After taking the *adamah* and creating the *ha adam,* we see that God is taking a piece of the *ha adam* and creating the *ish* and *ishah,* the man and the woman. God puts the human to sleep and takes a chunk out, and now there are two! The multiplying continues! "Be fruitful and multiply" is the continual mantra of the Genesis creation narrative and our calling to be co-creators with our God.

One final piece is that one of the best parts of this narrative is often hidden from plain sight. Genesis 2:10 – 14 has often caused people to go out in search of the location of the Garden of Eden over the years. It is slightly odd-sounding in the text how this geographical pericope about four rivers is stuck right in the middle of this origin story. Upon closer inspection, we see this moment is conveying the same message as the whole.

We learn that four rivers are flowing out of the garden where God places humanity: Pishon, Gihon, Tigris, and the Euphrates. These names translated from the Hebrew are *Increase, Bursting-Forth, Rapid, Fruitfulness.* Isn't this beautiful? Proliferation is baked into the whole thing. These four watery vessels of life flow out of this blossoming Garden of Eden where humanity is placed directly inside.

We cannot escape the message:

Be fruitful!
Multiply!
Create!
Expand!
Seeds, seed!
Shoots, shoot forth!
Increase!
Fill the Earth!
Germinate!
Grow!

If you and I live into our purpose here on the Earth, it is inevitable that all life and all materiality will flourish in the wake as the rivers of fruitfulness flow through us.

Respond & Reflect

Respond

→ *Take 1 hour this week and spend extra time in nature.*

Not for exercise. Not for a good place to study. Not to accomplish anything. Not to consume anything. Not to "use" time well. Visit a park, a nature preserve, or a hiking trail and attempt to rest in creation, with no agenda, for one hour.

Share any thoughts or photos from your experience with #GarbageTheologyBook

Reflect

What did this time stir within you?

Does the natural world feel like something you are connected to or estranged from?

Did you notice how efficient nature is? Did you notice, in nature, that there is nothing going to waste?

What is your personal waste story? In your life what has your relationship around waste been like?

Have you ever stopped to consider some of these ideas before? What stands out to you from this chapter?

Have you ever thought of waste as being outside of God's will for creation?

If we are made out of the ground, in the image of God, how might that change the ways we think about our relationship with creation?

Do you think that God's image inside each of us has something to say about what's inside of our trash bin? Do you think that our Creator is calling us to act on behalf of all this wastefulness?

Have you thought of God as a salvaging God before? What are some other Biblical stories you are familiar with that remind us of these Divine characteristics?

Garages, Basements, Attics, Sheds

Do not store up for yourselves treasures on Earth, where moth and rust consume and where thieves break in and steal; but store up for yourselves treasures in heaven, where neither moth nor rust consumes and where thieves do not break in and steal. For where your treasure is, there your heart will be also.
Matthew 6:19-21

If you want to see how many skeletons are in your waste closet, go check out your shed. If you haven't come to realize this principle yet, pay attention and you will:

If you have space, you'll fill it.

It's true. How many of us have empty rooms in our house? Empty garages? Empty sheds?
You see these *shed spaces* are where you really find out about people's theology of garbage. I've wondered if our sheds aren't embodied projections of an unreconciled fear of scarcity. (Lived out in the most abundant country on Earth!) The nasty truth of it is, everything in that shed will eventually be thrown away. Eventually you'll die, and maybe your friends or kids will take a few items, or some things will be sold... there will be a small shuffle of stuff as people take what is in your garage and make a small space in their basement for it. But in the end, the junk hauler is called up. He gets money, and the stuff gets tossed.

I've walked into basements and garages that would make Ariel's treasure cave look amateur!

Boxes, tools, excess building material, Christmas décor, trophies, clothes, outdated technology, gadgets and gizmos of plenty. I've cleaned out basements before of people who had lived in the same house for decades, and it was like walking through generations of manufacturing. Every shelf was like seeing the newest toys and techs of each era. Each had been used and then placed below to be forgotten. While upstairs, a new commercial played on the new TV.

One of my life goals is to get to the end of my days and have nothing. I imagine myself old and on my death bed as I hand off my very last possession... my baseball cap! But instead, just like that magic trash truck that comes and takes our garbage out of sight for us, these storage spaces act in a similar way. We can tuck away these items, not having to see them all the time, but yet still retain them... you know, just in case! There are homes and bedrooms and kitchens and cabinets and closets and attics full of just-in-cases!

At some point we must confront whether we possess our belongings, or our belongings possess us. Our yearning to possess seems intrinsically tied to our need for control. As it happens, our belongings can become mirrors reflecting our own deeper health or wounds. Yet, instead of confronting our shadows, we can easily point to the "hoarders" and proudly say, "Now that's bad!"

Practically, we are living in an era like none other in history, in which so many things have been manufactured and are out there in the world. Our homes, our streets, our workplaces, even our cars are filled with stuff. Just take extra notice today as you go about your routine at how many *things* there are. How much time do you already spend in a week shuffling through that basket in the bathroom, raking through that drawer for Q-tips, looking for your shoes in the bottom of your closet, hunting for your lunchbox in the kitchen cabinet? How much of our lives do we waste by simply having to slug our way forward through all the stuff? It's like trying to run in hip-high water. Do you live restrained by the things you purchased to set you free?

When Jesus calls his disciples into lifestyles of leaving everything behind and following him, it wasn't just because Jesus was in a hurry. Jesus calls us to shake loose from a lifestyle of possessions. He says not to worry about our lives and not store up treasure on Earth because he was tapping into a deeper truth. If only we'd take Jesus' words more seriously about not storing up junk on Earth, because it's absolutely true that the rust, moths, and junk haulers will eventually have their day with it!

Anyone on the street could rattle off proverbial sayings such as "money doesn't buy happiness." Yet, of course, remembering something isn't equated with knowing something. We remember lots of things we don't know. Jesus calls his followers to become less. And this inevitably became their great struggle. Jesus holds up a small child and tells us to become like children if we are to receive the kingdom. Following Jesus means leaving behind not only belongings and wealth but family and security. The monastics have been chanting this one for centuries.

There is something special that happens between a person and God when there is absolutely nothing in the way. It is like entering life.

How might we embrace small-living and small-lives in order to enter eternal life, today?

Here's an idea for that back yard shed: disassemble it and use the material to create raised beds in its place. Growing new tomatoes are way better than the old car battery under the rotting workbench that you never use. As for that garage, transform it into a community repair café!

Here's a challenge: get rid of some space. Less space is less stuff. *I promise.*

Respond

→ *Visit Repair.org to see how you can help promote and be an advocate for the right to repair.*

One great piece of legislation to support is the Right to Repair. This bill is meant to give the consumer a clear pathway and ability to access parts, tools, diagnostics, and documentation needed to repair. This is a huge step forward! This is something that you can support right now to make a difference. As consumers, we should all have the ability and way forward to repair the items we've purchased once they've broken. Acquiring the necessary information or parts should be part of the regular process of purchasing.

→ *Start a Repair Cafe!*

Ever just wanted a local place to go that would fix that broken toaster? Imagine having a local spot where you can take your bike, clothes, appliances, and even toys to be repaired? This is the idea behind a Repair Cafe. There are over 1,500 Repair Cafes around the world where handy people are doing their part, one broken household object at a time. These little shops are meant to be places where you can come and have items repaired or just hang out with a cup of coffee, help out, or engage in the learning process. Are you handy? Do you know others who might be good at this? Consider starting one in your garage! Simply start with getting the word out and opening up for a couple of hours on a Saturday. This is a great way to engage in a practical need that everyone has, and there are several good models of successful repair cafes out there. So many things just need a little tender loving care. [1]

Visit RepairCafe.org/en for inspiration in your own corner of the world

CHAPTER THREE

Heaven, Holy, Heresy

As you go, proclaim the good news, 'The Kingdom of heaven
has come near.
Matthew 10:7

Once upon a Spring, I found myself about to graduate from
college, falling in love with a certain someone, and discerning
what was going to be next in life. Although, like many of us
experience, there came a season of deconstructing that pre-
ceded building the new thing. During that period, I spent so
much time reflecting on questions such as: What *is* the
church? What exactly *is* a Christian? Out of all of these things
we say we need in order to *do* church, what would it look like
to simply *be* the church? The great things I had been learning
about the kingdom of God through my education really
seemed to be at odds with much of what I had experienced
the church to be.

Through fire, Earthquakes, and a whirlwind, I discovered a
still small voice. Abandoning the logical path, I found myself
graduating in May and moving to Germany in July. There in
the beautiful city of Mainz, I joined a team of amazing people
to help begin a church there called KiA Mainz. KiA stands for
Kirche in Aktion (Church in Action). There in the middle of
the city, we constructed a massive tent and spent a whole

week holding evening worship services, enjoying meals together, and during the day, we went out serving the city. We
spent each day that first week cleaning out filth-ridden
ponds, picking up trash off the street, feeding the homeless,
and baking food for local businesses. Literally, a big part of
launching this church was a group of us wading into a local
body of water and lugging out mounds of junk! As we went,
we announced, "The kingdom of heaven has come near." Is
there a better way to plant a church than putting on muddy
boots and gloves and embodying the kingdom of God in the
neighborhood? In the midst of all of this change, I found myself not only in culture shock from spatial displacement but in
the new kingdom of God culture shock. God was reconstruct-
ing church for me, just as it was being dismantled.

What on Earth Belongs in Heaven?

Jesus, in Matthew chapter 10, after having healed the sick,
raised the dead, cast out demons everywhere he went, turns
to his disciples and says, "*Your* turn!" He sends out 72 disciples in pairs and says, "As you go, proclaim the good news,
'The kingdom of heaven has come near.' Cure the sick, raise
the dead, cleanse the lepers, cast out demons. You received
without payment; give without payment."[1] There is a direct
link to the kingdom of heaven advancing and Jesus' disciples
bodily bringing it forth into the world!

Let that marinate.

If Jesus' "mission" could be summed up, it would be found in Mark 1:15, "The time is fulfilled, and the kingdom of God has come near; repent, and believe in the good news." Somehow, almost unbelievably, we often miss the core of Jesus' message: heaven coming to Earth, and us being reshaped for it.

Jesus continually uses the Greek imperative verb *metanoeite,* which means *"change your mind,"* (most commonly translated as *"repent"*).

Put simply, what we believe about heaven should become incarnate in the ways we think and the ways we live here on Earth. Our hands ought to be crafting heavenly creations. Our feet moving in heavenly directions. Our households a reflection of heaven-like spaces.

We visit the lonely because we believe there are no lonely people in heaven.
We tend to the sick because we believe there are no sick people in heaven.
We feed the hungry because we believe there is no hunger in heaven.
We pick up trash because we believe there is no trash in heaven!
Our work in the world is the embodying of the kingdom of heaven on Earth.

Imagine with me a place... that has no packaging. Imagine food, just naked in all its glory, no plastic around it, no rubber bands holding stems of broccoli together, no boxes or preservative packets needed. Imagine a place with no Styrofoam plates or single-use plastic cups. Imagine there were no landfills full of toothbrushes and bottles and bags that we happened to use once, then threw away. Imagine there were no dumpsters or trash cans at all because in this place, there is simply nothing to throw away. Every item is real, redeemed, and purposeful.

Imagine Heaven.

The work of the church must involve imagining and then embodying heaven here on Earth.

This is the work Jesus was doing day in and day out through his ministry, and we have only a percentage of the teachings and parables Jesus shared with his followers about what "the kingdom of heaven is like." He was continually sharing glimpses of heaven to those who had ears to hear. Jesus was consistently challenging his disciples with these parables and inviting them to participate in these heavenly narratives. These parables about seeds (Mark 4) and servants (Matthew 25) and parties (Matthew 22) are Jesus calling us to participate in the imagining.

Jesus was inviting us to hear and receive the fundamental elements of the kingdom of heaven! Not because we were going to go there one day and needed a travel brochure four gospels long, but Jesus taught us this because it is absolutely essential for the heavenly work we are here on Earth to do! We are here to see how heaven can break into our lives, our city, and our world. Just as the prayer states, "God's will be done on Earth as it is in heaven." Jesus teaches us this prayer so that we might daily begin learning to have kingdom posture in our world... so that in our praying for heaven, we might find it in the most unexpected place: Earth.

Therefore, we see why we must first talk about heaven before we can deal with our trash. Because once we understand that us joining in with God's mission on Earth is about our co-laboring in the renewal of all things, rather than the escaping from all things, we embrace a posture of resurrection in all that we do and in all that we touch.

I wonder, what if heaven is zero-waste?

What if living into our citizenship as the people of heaven looks like taking care of each and every bit of creation that comes through our hands? What if we become a people who "practice resurrection" as the great Wendell Berry would say?[2] What if we are to be the people who are up-to heaven on Earth? What if there's no room in heaven for waste? And what if we began to embody this new place, right now, here?

Holy God, Holy People, Holy Everything

The LORD spoke to Moses, saying:
Speak to all the congregation of the people of Israel and say
to them: You shall be holy, for I the LORD your God am holy.
- Leviticus 19:1-2

This chapter in Leviticus begins by God letting us in on who
we're meant to be. God says, "Be holy for I the LORD your God am
holy." If the Torah teaches us anything, it's that holy living has
something to say about *everything.* No topic, no thing, no idea,
no movement, no decision, no relationship is outside the scope
of holy living. Just in this chapter of Leviticus alone, we cover:

Our relationship with our parents
How we rest
Ways in which we eat
Ways we are harvesting our fields
The kinds of words we use
Things we take with our hands
How we treat our animals
How we sow our seeds
How we have sex
And how we are treating the foreigners in our land

Later, there are even guidelines about our sideburns! Because if you're going to follow God, you might as well do it
in style.

It would seem nothing escapes the purview of following this holy God. Holiness touches everything.

That's fittingly what the term is about... *wholeness.* That's what this entire journey as God's people is about, "*What does it mean to become whole?*" Because our God is whole.

Wholeness is in many ways the opposite of waste. When the ecosystems and environments are whole, in that they have all their original parts, working as they're designed to, it is the antithesis of wastefulness.

So, what does this mean for us that holiness touches everything? That all of creation is set apart for God? Is it any coincidence that our God who is whole weaves together a beautiful creation that is itself a reflection of wholeness? Should we be surprised that everything is connected? Creation is wired together. We've been warned for years that when the honeybees finally go, humans may not be that far behind.[3] We are not separate parts, un-connected, in our goings about on this planet. We are all intertwined for the life, beauty, and fruitfulness of the world.

One of our first errors was believing "dominion"[4] was about having power over creation rather than lovingly caring for creation. In other words, it isn't about having permission to manipulate creation how we please, but that we have the opportunity as humans to love creation as God does. Part of the opportunity to enjoy the garden is getting to tend to it! Heart-holiness always translates into hand-holiness, because we are a holy people who belong to a holy God.

What if there is nothing that God doesn't care about? As my wife, Emily, so eloquently puts it, "I dare you to name something that doesn't matter to God."

What if when I go to the store, I do my shopping as a holy person belonging to a holy God? What if I make purchases witnessing to the truth that everything belongs? What if I live into my world believing that God doesn't waste, so I can seek to be zero-waste, too?

Our life here, by design, is meant to be a reflection of a God who comes and makes things whole. And that changes just about everything, doesn't it?

The heavens are telling the glory of God; and the firmament proclaims his handiwork. Day to day pours forth speech, and night to night declares knowledge. There is no speech, nor are there words; their voice is not heard; yet their voice goes out through all the Earth, and their words to the end of the world.
- **Psalm 19:1-4**

Before we turn the page, it must be pointed out that there has been a great wedge often placed between the Christian and nature. Long-standing misinterpretations of Scripture and fear-based homilies are still echoing from years gone by. But the people of God were never meant to live in opposition to the land or God's creatures or necessarily anything created from it. We've historically wasted too much time not taking care of creation with excuses such as "being of the world" or "loving the flesh" or "worshiping nature."

So, for the sake of a moment of clarity —
No, we should not have idols.
No, our God is not equivalent to creation.
Yes, we worship God alone.

We are creatures made into the image of God. We are reflections of this divine relationship.

Creation informs us of the nature of God as water reflects an image.

Yet somehow, in our worries about becoming pantheist or hedonist... it was a different heresy altogether that became Christianity's Achilles' heel.

Heresy

But be doers of the word, and not merely hearers who deceive themselves. For if any are hearers of the word and not doers, they are like those who look at themselves in a mirror;

for they look at themselves and, on going away, immediately forget what they were like. But those who look into the perfect law, the law of liberty, and persevere, being not hearers who forget but doers who act—they will be blessed in their doing. If any think they are religious, and do not bridle their tongues but deceive their hearts, their religion is worthless. Religion that is pure and undefiled before God, the Father, is this: to care for orphans and widows in their distress, and to keep oneself unstained by the world.

- James 1:22-27

I'm sitting in a local coffee shop right now, and as I look up at the wall, it says "Zero-Waste." Here this label means they have made steps to prevent anything from going to a landfill. Everything here is either recycled or composted. It's a great business model! As a pastor, my question is always: if a coffee shop can do this, why can't the church? How is it that all these little businesses I frequent on a weekly basis seem to be catching on to this, but the gathering places of the people of God, our church buildings and institutions, often can't seem to do this well? Why has it been such a leap for us to connect our holiness theology with our hands and not just our hearts? Why is it a challenge to see that everything matters to God? If God is up to anything in the world, isn't God going into every corner of our world and breathing life? Maybe a better question is: could Gnosticism still be alive and well?

Gnosticism is an early church heresy that adhered to the belief that our spirits are what matters to God, not our bodies. It adhered to the belief that things of the world, the flesh, matter itself, was more or less evil, and that if we *know the right things,* we can find salvation of the spirit.

While this was an ordeal for early Christians, this doctrine may be more of a challenge for Western Christianity today. Escapist theology has infiltrated Christian doctrine in the west for some time now. Much of the gospel we hear today has to do with leaving the world behind, wiping the soil off our feet, and thinking, talking, and singing about those golden streets way up high. Could this be the new seeds of Gnosticism?

What is the fruit of a Gnostic gospel?

It is a gospel that has become ethereal rather than tangible.
It is a gospel more concerned with leaving rather than redeeming.
It has its sights only on tomorrow rather than today.
It is the propagation of future hope for our souls without hope for the present reality of our bodies and our planet.
It is a soul without a body.
This sort of gospel fundamentally misunderstands the incarnation of Christ on Earth.

Gnosticism today has created a version of Christianity that is willing to watch the world burn while hypocritically confessing Jesus the Christ, the Incarnation of the Triune God, as Lord. God himself has taken on a body and lived in a particular place so that we may know the resurrection of all things. God is in the business of redeeming everything.[5]

If God isn't in our fingers and toes and everything they touch and everywhere they walk, is God really then in our hearts? If our sanctification isn't extending to the entire planet, is it really then entire? Are we just the updated remodeled version of Gnosticism? If we are just waiting to "Fly Away," unwavered by what is happening and believing God doesn't care about the waste in our world, I would venture to say that our theology is a bit like garbage.

Creation, Incarnation, Sanctification

He is the image of the invisible God, the firstborn of all creation; for in him all things in heaven and on Earth were created, things visible and invisible, whether thrones or dominions or rulers or powers—all things have been created through him and for him. He himself is before all things, and in him all things hold together.
- **Colossians 1:15-17**

"Jesus took on flesh and moved into the neighborhood," to quote the late Eugene Peterson's paraphrase of John 1. As God comes to be born on the Earth, walk these dusty paths, eat this gritty and succulent food, craft out of wood and metal with his hands, his very presence redeems all he encounters. The incarnation of Jesus teaches us about the sanctity of all of life and materiality. In doing this, it is disclosed that flesh belongs and so does everything in the neighborhood.

As an ordained minister, I've officiated many weddings for dear friends over the years. One piece of the liturgy for matrimony in the Church of the Nazarene[6] always strikes a chord with me. It states that "Christ adorned and sanctified marriage with his presence and miracle at the wedding in Cana." It is through the miraculous presence of Jesus on Earth we see what all has been made holy. Through Jesus' incarnational presence there at this event in Cana of Galilee, marriage itself becomes sanctified. When God enters an environment that environment is transformed. [7] [8]

Jesus' presence in the world becomes the inaugural big bang of heaven breaking into Earth upon every room he enters. Death and suffering vanish away in the very presence of God. What choice do they have? When God physically enters a building, death has to wait at the door.

Sometimes as pastors, we get all sorts of questions about Scripture: Is Lazarus still alive somewhere out there? Do those Jesus healed or raised from the dead later become ill and die again? Of course, they did. But what this tells us is crucial to understand. We learn about the importance of the present for Jesus.

We are reminded through Jesus' healing actions in the world that he deeply cares about the present state of suffering.

Jesus healed people in the present, despite the fact that their bodies would continue to decay. Love always acts upon present suffering; it never shrugs its shoulders at the pain of our neighbor and says, "They were just going to die anyway." Jesus especially didn't look the leper in the eye and say, "You know I'm coming back soon! So, we'll see you on the other side, okay?" Jesus wasn't simply encouraging folks with promises of a better tomorrow but was participating in the redemption of the present.

Jesus' first miracle in Cana may be my favorite of all the miracles listed in John. Not only does the miracle itself keep the party going, but how powerful is it that the first divine interruption with the natural world we see Jesus do is with something so Earthy as water and wine? This action by Jesus did not heal anyone. It was not fixing something that was broken. If this hadn't happened, the wedding would still have gone on, and everyone would have been fine. Jesus' action, influenced by his loved ones, was a glimpse of the pleasure God takes in creation. And that pleasure is directly connected to dancing with friends and enjoying the fruits of the Earth.

The Incarnation is our Creator's way of finally reminding us of the real true sanctity in all of creation... that it is in fact, very good. This world we live in is designed to be *tov*. It is through the person of Jesus and his 33 years walking this place that we ultimately rediscover the sanctity of all of it. He walks through streets and homes and gardens. He's baptized in water, eats the fish, breaks the bread, drinks the wine, and writes in the dirt. Jesus touches those with leprosy, re-attaches a soldier's ear, and lifts up a bleeding woman.

So before we begin declaring God is *here* and not *there*. Before we assuredly stand to say that *this ground is holy,* and *that ground is not.* We may want to reflect on the lyrics sung by King David, "The Earth is the Lord's and all that is in it."[9]

In our haste to say, "This is worthless, and this is valuable," I wonder... what if one person's trash is our God's treasure? In our efforts to create separations, to divvy out and say, "This belongs, and this doesn't," I wonder... what if God is a garbage worker?
In declaring, "This is trash, and this has value," I wonder... what if all matter matters?

What if waste was never the plan?

Diapers and Dryers

Therefore, since we are receiving a kingdom that cannot be shaken, let us give thanks, by which we offer to God an acceptable worship with reverence and awe; for indeed our God is a consuming fire.
- Hebrews 12:28-29

One of the key characteristics that differ in this "heaven on Earth" eschatology is the work of our hands. The most popular view of heaven as a place we are escaping to lets us off the hook for what happens to all this down here on Earth. If we continue to misinterpret fire as solely God's means of destroying rather than God's message about purification, phrases such as, "It will all burn anyway," will inevitably lead us to, ironically, hell on Earth.

Living intentionally into heaven on Earth has led me elbows deep in waste. For many years, this was literally baby poop! Let me assure you, only my beliefs about holiness and heaven could have seen me through our four and a half years of cloth diapering! Although cloth diapers aren't a viable choice for every parent, disposable diapers are one of the key items some of us can avoid using to make a big difference. In 2017, the EPA reported that an estimated 4.2 million tons of disposable diapers were thrown away in America alone.[10] We toss upwards of 20 billion disposable diapers in the landfill each year! At about 7 diapers on average being used in one day for one baby, this is an enormous hit to our landfills and an enormous hit to our wallet. These diapers are lined in plastic, and today, it's still-to-be-determined how many hundreds of years it will take for these diapers to "decompose." It doesn't matter how old you are, if you were put in disposable diapers as a child, that "stuff" is still out there somewhere! In fact, without being exposed to sun and air, even many of the "eco-friendly" diapers will unfortunately not decompose much quicker than regular disposable brands.

If we believe that the people of God are called into a redemptive relationship of serving and keeping all matters of creation, then we should strongly observe how each choice, including what diapers we use, is aligned with the will of God. Does it advance the kingdom of heaven, or not?

Another tangible living-heaven-on-Earth change we've embraced over the years is not having a dryer. Inspired by author and speaker, Matthew Sleeth, Emily and I decided never to have a dryer when we got married over a decade ago. Using a dryer has a hefty carbon footprint; it wastes large amounts of energy while cutting the lifespan of your clothing in half. Because of this, we've been able to keep our wardrobe for many years longer than usual. Although this lifestyle has not stopped many gracious folks and sweet neighbors over the years from having pity on us as our undies hang dry on the front porch! We have had numerous people attempt to actually give us a dryer! One of the odd things we've had to learn is that it can take a great deal of intentionality to stick with your values in a world of material abundance. It is inevitable that the further you live into the kingdom of God, the odder you will appear to those who aren't seeing through your lens. It will be challenging to remain a course when your culture attempts to make things as easy as possible for you otherwise.[11]

One of our current local initiatives to eliminate waste has been being involved at our daughter's elementary school. We've helped create a "Green Team" there and implement school-wide recycling. A funny moment happened one day when my wife was chatting with someone at the school about living eco-friendly. They asked Emily, "Would you really refuse a drink somewhere if you had forgotten to bring your cup that day?" To which my wife smiled and responded, "That's true! Refusing a drink is the best way to remember to bring your cup!"

This interaction, though amusing, is at the heart of what it will require for us all to make the first steps. At what point do we care enough that our values affect our choices? Because really, if what you believe doesn't change the way you live, even if it's inconvenient, do you really believe it? If we cannot begin with something as small as forgoing a drink, how will we ever address the larger issues facing our hurting planet? Living "green" is not convenient, at least not as convenient as not living green. Just like anything worth standing for, it requires effort to stand. For us to move beyond the coffee cup to indeed restoring God's created order to the planet, we will have to stand with great intentionality, because at every turn, it will just be easier to use the appliance, or disposable diapers, or single-use item. This sort of reorientation and repentance is not a minor one but will be a test at our core as it pushes on the very things that make our lives comfortable. We often don't realize how much we love our comforts until there is a threat of losing them.

Maybe you're thinking, "I have worked my entire life for these comforts and luxuries." Just like many of the Jews of Jesus' day struggled with his message then, because it felt like an upheaval of everything they had built. The infrastructure, the rituals, the sacrificing, the temple itself, following Jesus meant all that would change. I wonder if sometimes we can hardly entertain a theology that is different than our own because if we did… well, that could mean more discomfort than we think we could bear.

But there is good news here as we continually become reoriented and bent toward the kingdom of God. The ongoing, healing, transformative, and sanctifying presence of God in our lives is at work in us one day at a time. And the things that were initially very challenging begin to become second nature for us. This is important to keep in mind as we begin making the small life changes of caring for creation. The "repenting" part will always be the hardest. The turning around and moving in another direction will never feel natural until we've been doing it for a while.

And eventually, it doesn't just become "normal" as you're realigning your lifestyle to reflect the coming kingdom of God, it becomes joyous.

Respond & Reflect

Respond

→ *Hang dry all your laundry for one week.*

Sometimes our machines can make parts of our lives so easy that trying things differently just feels unnecessary and over-whelming. Yet, oddly enough, trying new ways of doing famil-iar tasks for a few days can sometimes surprise us with how normative it can become.

For one week, unplug that dryer, unload your washer, and find creative ways to hang your laundry! If you don't have a drying rack or a clothesline, hang sheets over doors, the back of chairs, on hangers, front porches, and back decks. Try it! What have you got to lose?

If you knew that changing this one habit could drastically al-ter your carbon footprint (and save you money), could you keep it up?

Post a picture of your hanging laundry with ...

#GarbageTheologyBook

Reflect

What stood out to you during this exercise?

How did this practice challenge you in unexpected ways?

What other similar alterations in your day-to-day life might you make to positively impact our world?

Have you thought of heaven before as it's described here?

Does thinking about heaven as something being established on Earth excite you or bother you?

How might this picture of heaven confront the ways we treat our belongings?

How much of our waste crisis in the world do you think is driven by being discontent with what we already own?

Would you ever consider not remodeling your home for the sake of the kingdom of heaven on Earth?

Have you ever thought about waste being a belief system? Do you think waste was ever supposed to exist?

Undo

For about the last century, it would seem that society has been making decisions by one single question: "Can we do this?" Yet, all along we should have been asking, "Should we do this?" In the end, we're left with the work of undoing wrongs that should have never been unleashed. The future work of caring for creation is learning how to undo much of what we've done. Plastic is the perfect example of such a problem.

First, let it be clear. Plastic has saved countless lives. Plastic represents a leap forward in society and industry. There is no doubt about the good that has occurred in the world due to the advancements of plastics! But the danger of any new advancement is first, that we would grow complacent and not continue to reinvent and make these inventions better. And second, that this new development would be exploited by greedy enterprises. Fast-forward years later and creation is inundated with plastic. We found something that was cheap to produce and could be fabricated for almost any job, and it didn't matter what happened after that.

Today, we know it is highly probable that plastic is inside us.

A 2019 study revealed that we consume around a credit card's worth of plastic each week. This happens as plastic eventually becomes brittle and breaks apart into smaller and smaller fragments, becoming irretrievably a part of our water and soil. We live in a time of plastic saturation. Even when plastic is recycled, it still exists in a new form, leaking into the world.

It floats in our oceans and enters our water stream every time we wash our polyester yoga pants. Plastic is eaten by fish and then consumed by us. It has irretrievably infiltrated our ecosystem on an immense scale. But just like many other issues that aren't in front of our faces and visible to us, we care too little. If bottled water is convenient and quenches our thirst, that's all we need to know, right? But little do we realize that the water inside this bottle may also have plastic inside it. This never-ending production of plastic is causing environmental havoc on our ecosystems and us. [1]

Whenever I pull up to clean a job site, the first thing I typically do is go around and pick up every plastic bottle I can find. The most I've ever picked up at one job site is two 42 gallon-size trash bags full of plastic bottles! This is an absurd reality occurring at almost any worksite I've been to. A week later, I'll often arrive and, unbelievably, do it all over again. We now know that enough plastic bottles are thrown away each year to circle the Earth four times. This is an immense scale, especially for a type of waste that will not decompose but only contaminate. [2]

These sorts of places where bottles are just tossed onto the ground help put the problem in perspective even more. This is essentially what is happening in the landfill. Plastic lying in the ground never decaying. Out of sight, out of mind. It's hard to comprehend that plastic straw you used as a child still being out there somewhere. Sure, it's probably in microscopic pieces about now, but it's still there... a permanent part of our planet. That toothbrush you were brushing baby teeth with... still out there. That plastic cup from that one single visit to your favorite restaurant (*by the way, if this is the case, get a new favorite restaurant!*) is still out there somewhere. Plastic doesn't go anywhere; it stays. Plastic is a huge problem in our world, especially one-time, single-use products.

Recycling plastic is somewhat a myth as-well. Depending on what sort of recycling companies are near you, many times only certain plastics get recycled. And sometimes, it isn't necessarily every part of that item. On a recent tour of our recycling center here in town, we discovered that just about the only plastic that was recycled there were bottles! Not containers, lids, small pieces, or other plastic "oddities," but mostly just bottles. This was incredibly despairing news after spending years thinking we were recycling, when in fact, these items made it to the landfill anyway. Similarly, in Nashville, there are few spots to "recycle" items such as batteries or lightbulbs, and typically you'll have to do a little driving around town just to do it. Although upon further research, we realized that these batteries and bulbs aren't actually being recycled at all. They are simply being "disposed of properly," which is a good thing, but a far cry from the recycling that we often think we are engaged in.

The dirty truth is, even if our plastic bottle we gladly recycle makes it all the way through and is sorted and bailed... some entity has to buy it. Unfortunately, the world's largest used-plastic purchaser, China, isn't nearly as interested in purchasing as much as they used to be. Recently, China's contamination standards have squeezed even tighter (you can see why it's so important to clean that peanut butter jar beforehand).

While this is causing mass graves of plastic worldwide, it is also spurring new creativity to the problem as the waste piles up in our yards, and people finally take notice. How might we be committed to making the small life changes of our bottles, bags, and toothbrushes?

More people and businesses are beginning to think about these issues and use compostable dinnerware and single-use products made from "eco" material. Although, just switching from one single-use product to another will never move us to solve the environmental impact of such wastefulness. Some of these "eco-friendly" options already require more water, energy and chemicals to manufacture than their plastic counterparts. And although eco-dinnerware like this may be labeled "compostable," it often doesn't break down very easily in a compost. Some composters don't want them because it lessens the value of the compost. [3] [4]

At the end of the day, recycling, ironically, is not the answer. Reducing your waste footprint is always the best way forward. Yes, we should recycle every item we possibly can! But if we want to take care of creation, the real solution is changing and reducing our consumption habits.

The real solution is just getting a real spoon.

How might we be so bold as to refuse these plastic and single-use products in the first place? How can we reorient our lives toward not needing these products that are harming the

Earth, our common home? We've gone thousands of years without most of these "necessities." I believe we can do without them still. We are innovative enough to not go backward as a society but find a better pathway forward to a cleaner, holier tomorrow.

In 2019, the European Union passed a Single-Use Plastics Directive that bans the use of straws, cutlery, plates — and so on — that alternatives already exist for. This is a huge step forward as the E.U. will set a hopeful example for the rest of the world. Living outside of these paradigms of waste should not be an overwhelming task, but it ultimately does require our leaders to take legislative action against these harmful societal practices that plague our homes, streets, landfills, and especially, oceanic life.[1]

Unless we relearn ancient ways of cloth diapering and drinking out of real cups, we will only continue to drastically fill our planet with waste. But not just any old waste, irreconcilable waste. How might the people of God lead the way as stewards of this holy ground?

Jesus wore cloth diapers... that's all you really need to know.

Respond

→ *Make your own plastic-free "Go" bag!*

Find a backpack or a crate and stock it with items that you use on a weekly basis that will help you avoid single-use plastics.

- Fork, spoon, and knife
- Cloth napkins and towels
- A to-go container
- Bamboo straws
- Cloth grocery bags
- A coffee mug
- A mason jar with a lid

Get creative!

Snap a photo of your kit and share it —

#GarbageTheologyBook

CHAPTER FOUR

Seeing the Re-Cycle

Blurring the Waste Lines

One of the first things we learn as children are of course the rules.

Do this, not that.
Never touch an outlet.
Always wear pants in public.
Eat all your veggies.
Don't hit your sister!
(Depending on your context these tend to differ.)

We come out of the womb and into the world and life is first given to us as a set of binaries. We say, "This is good, and this is bad." These are invaluable lessons for us to learn early on. The boundaries are essential for our development and our growth. The lines give us a safe framework to mature in early on. But as it happens, the more we mature the more the lines seem to blur, don't they? Because as we grow and expand, our minds and hearts grow and expand. We see that there is so much more going on in the world than we first knew. The issues and the politics are complicated (Of course they are! Otherwise why would there be so much controversy!). The world is more complex and diverse than we ever thought. This is the natural evolution and change of awakening and maturing.

Perhaps it's what the Apostle Paul touches on in Ephesians as he refers to, "the eyes of your heart enlightened."[1] It's that we come to know more of the mystery that is the glory of the resurrected Christ alive in our world.

This enlightening of the eyes of your heart occurs as we further come to know the image of God. Early on we receive these nice stories from the Bible that make uncomplicated coloring pages and puzzles, but later on, we realize that the pieces don't fit together as well as we thought they would. Actually, the more we try to understand the mystery of God with our dualistic minds, it all just seems to blow up in our faces.

Because, well...

What is a virgin birth?
How is it that Jesus is completely Divine and completely human?
How is it that God is Trinity? How can Three be One?
How is it that this Eucharistic bread and wine are the body and blood of Jesus the Christ?

None of this "makes sense." Yet, trusting these mysterious tensions are by very definition what it means to have faith. And faith rarely speaks in the language of binaries.

But still, for whatever reason, we are a people who love our categories and boxes. When life is binary it's just more comfortable, right? Life is just more simple when we can name this as "this" and that as "that."

Waste is the product of binaries.

We make sense of the waste in our culture, especially in the west, because we can easily label things. This is garbage and that is not. This is trash and this is useful. Our sanctioned trash-binaries help us give justification to landfills full of "not-goods."

We like to think the fabric and DNA of the universe is wired out of a system of rules that make things clear...

Black or White.
Up or Down.
Here or There.
In or out... Right?

Yet, if you have happened to follow any number of scientific discoveries in the last several years, scientists have found quite the opposite. The deeper scientists investigate into the very material that all of creation is made from, the subatomic places in every hand and every table and every chair, nothing seems to fit our binary playground. Just do a quick search for Gluons, or Quarks, or Higgs boson! Some particles even disappear in one place and reappear in another, and others can exist in two separate places at the same time![2] The sub-atomic material that every single thing is made from is anything but plain and simple.

If who we are at the root is made up of such a non-binary mystery, then isn't it probable that the rest of life might follow this non-dualistic mysterious path? Could it be that we just made these categories up because our view of life was just a little too simple, adolescent, or elementary to understand the truth of God's wholly interconnected creation?

Whenever we try to place a person or bit of creation in a box it naturally tries to break out! It's the reason why our enemy can become our friend once we've met them face to face and seen the nuance in their lives and stories. It's the reason we fall in love with one person and not another. It's the reason one person has a green thumb, and another's second-nature is making budgets and spreadsheets. There is an unmistakable mystery to life and creation. Yet every piece and every part still seem to have its place in the whole.

What is easier than placing the world in categories? The hard work is actually loving everyone and everything despite the lines we've drawn. Categories attempt to gate in our love, but the kingdom of heaven always transcends these chains and shackles we clasp onto God's loving presence.

Symbolic

This is the universal symbol for recycling. You can be anywhere in the world, see this symbol and know what it means. Take a moment and look at it. It is something that you see so much you may not see it at all.

There is no beginning. There is no end. If something is held within it, it stays within... because there is no exit, there is no without. What goes around comes back around here.

It endlessly flows clockwise. This one direction. Like a river.

In the middle, in the negative space, is a triangle. As it is a triangle, three arrows flip to point at the next arrow. This is the necessary maneuver. The change. The dance. This dance continues and continues as the arrows flow around and around.

It doesn't take long to notice some Trinitarian symbolism in the image. This isn't just a trash man's projection on God, it is an excavation of something set deep within the heart of creation for us to grab hold of. A thumbprint of our Creator in creation. It's no coincidence that universally we've latched on to this symbol to recognize recycling. It is the very idea of redemption and reuse and renewal. We are all inherently drawn to this saving idea. It's in our very identity that we would want redemption everywhere for everyone and everything. That nothing would be wasted!

The Trinitarian flow that continues from the love of Father, Son and Holy Spirit *should* remind us of the very flow between the Divine, the Divine image bearers called humans, and the humus that sustains us. We ourselves are drawn into this eternal flow, this dance that happens on the ground that we stand. All of creation is within this triangle, and whether you want to mistreat, misuse, or discard it, it's still there. But the more we act as if we can do whatever we want with the world, the more struggle we will be in as we attempt to swim against the flow or move counterclockwise to the universe!

What if there's no leaving the triangle just as there is no jumping to another planet?
What if there's no exit ramp here? But just the continual choice to be a part of the advancing the kingdom of heaven, living into this divine triune dance... or not.

CHAPTER FIVE

The Hells of Waste

The Earth dries up and withers, the world languishes and withers; the heavens languish together with the Earth. The Earth lies polluted under its inhabitants; for they have transgressed laws, violated the statutes, broken the everlasting covenant. Therefore a curse devours the Earth, and its inhabitants suffer for their guilt; therefore the inhabitants of the Earth dwindled, and few people are left.

Isaiah 24:4-6

Gehenna

It's a cloudy afternoon as I back the truck into the drive. Immediately I noticed the large mountain range made up of couches, mattresses, dressers, clothes, televisions, and kitchenware in the yard awaiting my arrival. This is more here than I expected. The work order simply read "some rubbish in the yard." Understatement of the year! As I begin to wade my way into the trash, I become aware of the smell. Once you've danced with the trash devil as long as I have you develop certain senses. It's akin to having a "spidey-sense" except nowhere near as cool. After years of doing this, I can recognize the smell of a roach-infested house immediately. Sure enough, as soon as I caught their scent, I saw them scurrying in my peripheral vision. They were running for their survival, and I thought about running for mine! They are in literally everything. I kick over a dresser and hundreds run for cover! This is an infestation. Now I'm realizing hardly anything here can be salvaged. I work my way to the back of the house and open the back door. As my hand turns the knob and I cautiously crack the laundry room door open, a waterfall of roaches begins to rain down onto my arm! It was roach-mageddon.

There is trash everywhere.

Bugs everywhere.

Rotten food everywhere.

The stench of all that is unholy.

This place is hell.

One of the things I find most powerful in the gospels begins with the Greek word that we most commonly translate as hell: gehenna. This word literally translated is the valley (*ge*) of Hinnom (*henna*). This was a valley on the south side of Jerusalem where all the waste, filth and even dead animals were thrown and burned. This place was a landfill if there ever was one. If something was trash, this is where it was going. Continual fires and weeping and gnashing of teeth were actual descriptions of this place, as trash burned, and wild dogs made their rounds. Many even believed that this plot of ground had a curse on it.

Before this valley was the city dump, hundreds of years earlier, it was the place of worship called Topheth. Some of the kings of Judah were guilty of idol worship and sacrificing their children there in an effort to pay homage to foreign gods. We read in Jeremiah how God responds to this abomination,

> "And they go on building the high place of Topheth, which is in the valley of the son of Hinnom, to burn their sons and their daughters in the fire—which I did not command."[1]

So before Gehenna was a place for all waste it was where even human lives were wasted. Could there be a more appropriate name for this valley than hell?

Gehenna, Hell, *is* the actual place of waste.

I don't think there is any coincidence that Gehenna, this horrible place that gradually became the ultimate landfill and dump, was used heavily by the first-century Jewish community as a symbol for a hell-like place; the opposite of this Kingdom that Jesus announced was arriving. It begs the question, what if hell is what happens as creation gets wasted?

Waste at its core is something that has no value left in it. If something is truly waste, it can't be fixed or repaired. It can't be broken down for parts or recycled.

If it's actually waste, then it's unredeemable.

Let that sink in.

If we ascribe something as waste, that means it is useless, no longer good for anything, left only to be tossed in the fires of the valley of Hinnom.

And if our valleys full of waste are outside of God's created order, then this means the places like landfills, that hold all our unredeemed waste on Earth, have quite literally gone to hell. It is the place outside of God's created order.

Amazingly, creation itself, moving as it is originally ordered to do, is a waste-less place! When everything in creation goes about its life in fruitful use and reuse then even our deaths become part of heaven on Earth. Our bodies go into the ground to decay and create rich soil so that something else might grow. We are meant to produce kingdom compost, not waste!

In fact, the very order of our creation says that the ending of one thing becomes the beginning of the other. This cycle is divinely ordered... life, death, and new life. God is in the business of resurrection and in the beautiful creation story God blesses life and says, "*be fruitful and multiply!*"

So when creation finds its way into the landfills of our world, covered in plastic,
forever unused,
never decomposing,

never redeemed,
well, may I suggest that is what God dislikes the most?

Unredeemable garbage?

That's Hell.

What if, when we find ourselves participating in wasteful activities and over-consumption, we are actually participating in bringing a little bit of hell on Earth?

Jesus speaks to us about gehenna because Jesus is about the redemption of creation.

Jesus is the ultimate recycler.

If Jesus lived in your neighborhood I wonder if you might just see him digging through your trash...
"Yep, still good."
"Yeah, keeper!"
"Oh! I've got plans for this!"

Everywhere we see Jesus go he is in the business of redeeming, resurrecting, and calling to repentance. Reduce, reuse, recycle is part of what it means to be part of the kingdom of heaven!

The green triangle that we stick on the trash bins in the kitchen may have more to do with Trinitarian love than we've ever stopped to think about.

For some, this whole conversation may sound appalling: connecting God with our trash? But that's just the problem! We've taken God out of the dirt, out of the places and people God has so faithfully associated with and we've placed God clean and upright in the places we want God to be.

Are we still trying to make God in our own image? Or are we willing to be continually reshaped into the image of God, however holy, different, and mysterious that might be?

What if the warning of hell in our gospel has always been a warning about waste?
A warning to not squander everything good God has given us...
A warning to not waste our bodies, our homes, our time, our energy, our passion, our resources, our lives?
And a warning to not treat each other like waste?

What if just like heaven on Earth, we are also just as capable to participate in hell on Earth?

In Mark 9 Jesus speaks the familiar lines...

"And if your eye causes you to stumble, tear it out; it is better for you to enter the kingdom of God with one eye than to have two eyes and to be thrown into hell, where their worm never dies, and the fire is never quenched."[2]

Jesus is using "Gehenna" to call attention to that place that everyone would have been familiar with, the place where all waste goes. These verses are among some of the most graphic words we find in the gospels... should we cut off parts of our body in order that we might be saved? Jesus uses such shocking words for a reason. Jesus wants you to hear the importance of this message.

Could it be that what needs to be "thrown away" are the very things that cause us to live wasteful lives?

The entirety of creation is quite literally finding its way toward "Gehenna" today. If we don't take drastic measures of eliminating the right things... everything may find its way into the flames.

Trying to Respire

Now the man knew his wife Eve, and she conceived and bore Cain, saying, "I have produced a man with the help of the LORD." Next she bore his brother Abel. Now Abel was a keeper of sheep, and Cain a tiller of the ground.
- **Genesis 4:1-3**

The story of Cain and Abel is one that almost everyone knows. Sometimes I wonder if "Am I my brother's keeper?" isn't the most memorized in Scripture! This story is full of meaning for us in our conversation here. Could this be an ancient warning about humanity's tendency towards over-consumption and avarice?

The story goes that Eve initially has two sons. Her first son she names Cain and her second son, Abel. Cain in Hebrew is *qayin*, it means "possession." Abel, (*hebel*) means "breath."

Abel was a keeper of sheep, and Cain was a servant of the ground. All was well until the time came for offerings to God. What follows in the few verses of Genesis 4 is a mysterious narrative about God "regarding" Abel's offering but not Cain's. So what's the deal, Lord? Why does this happen? We are left to speculate around what causes God to regard one and not another. Even the term for regard, *sha`ah*, just means "to look or gaze at." We can't help but wonder, was one offering withholding while the other was given freely with open hands? Did one offering keep the best while the other was released as easily as a breath?

The story comes to a swift ending with a bloody murder. One brother dares to take, to possess, the other's very... breath.

Our tendency toward greed, avarice, jealousy, revenge, lust, possessing it all for ourselves... is almost as old as we are. We have historically been a people more concerned with what we can take and consume over what we are able to give.

The story of Cain and Abel has something very tangible to teach us about how we are to live... if we can receive it. Our relationship with God and with each other only thrives when we are able to breathe. Isn't this what we end up relearning every single day? Every time we inhale, we must exhale, every time we exhale, we must inhale. Every day we relearn that to live is to die. We remember that to lose our life is to find it. Jesus seemed to think this was an important point. But

Cain is already reiterating the sin of just a chapter ago! He takes life into his own hands.

But life has never been something we can take, only receive. And then we are simply invited to give everything back over as an offering to our God who has given us life. Life can only be lived as we breathe... the act of receiving the free air into our lungs and releasing it back as a gift to every growing thing. What then happens? The grass, the flowers, the herbs, the trees then transform and returns it back to us!

It is this re-cycle flow imprinted in the universe that announces to us what love actually looks like. Is it any coincidence that the very name of God we find in the Hebrew, YHWH is originally unspeakable? The very name is compared to the very sound of breathing![3] How often has our God shared this message for us? Ultimately, God joins us in the flesh through the person of Jesus to teach us this.

But the moment that we become more interested in possessing than with breathing...that is when it all begins to fall apart. That is the moment we take our brother's life. That is the moment we suffocate.

A Word on Judgement

"Do not judge, and you will not be judged; do not condemn, and you will not be condemned. Forgive, and you will be forgiven; give, and it will be given to you. A good measure, pressed down, shaken together, running over, will be put into

your lap; for the measure you give will be the measure you get back."
- **Luke 6:37-38**

What comes out of you comes back to you. What you put in you get out. What you've invested in you'll receive a return.

Give freely, Jesus says, because freely you have received.
Inflow outflow.
Inhale exhale.
Everything we've needed to know in a breath.

The more we clench our fists the less control we have.

The more we throw away the more wasteland this place becomes.

This mystery has always been as close as a mirror.

If we trash our world, our world will trash us.

If we protect
tend
watch
love our world...
We receive love in return.

What if that which we've put into the Earth, the Earth sprouts back out for us?

What if we spray pesticides and we get cancer?

What if we treat our livestock like objects for our gratification and our greed results in illness and permanently altering our atmosphere?

What if we leverage the soil to make us wealthy and it gives us thistles in return?

What if we throw our natural resources away at an unprecedented rate and our ecosystem gets thrown away too?

What if Genesis 3, the fall, is not about God cursing us, but about a brokenness between us and the Earth? What if this is a story about us breaking the relationship with God and creation by assuming, we can consume everything?

What if this "fall" is about the naturally occurring consequences when humanity attempts to become the god of ourselves?

The measure you give will be the measure you get back.

Choking from the Fires

Breathing is sacred. The divine air once breathed into our lungs to give us life is still moving into the atmosphere today. We could even think of breathing as sacramental as Jesus himself came and filled his lungs in the same way we do every day. I wonder, could there be a more profaning act against our Creator than to trash the very air we breathe?

One of the places I've had my share of skepticism in the past came whenever someone spoke about air pollutants. Growing up in the rolling green hills of Tennessee clean air seemed as accessible as a tree to climb. When people talked about smog or air that was supposedly dangerous it always sounded absurd. Even later as an adult living in Nashville I often secretly doubted the "air quality alert" warnings that flashed on the highway. "The air today looks like the air yesterday," I thought. "I can inhale just as well today as I've always been able to!" Yet, to our demise, this is another illusion in the unseen world of waste.

While this issue may be worse in some areas of the world than others or may feel distant to us, we are all affected by it in some capacity. Whether you live in western states, where in the winter there are larger proportions of nitrate particles from driving motor vehicles, or if you live in eastern states where you are subject to higher levels of sulfate particles emitted by coal-fired power plants, this is all our air.

We must all breathe this air to live. [4] [5]When there is trash saturated into the air we breathe, our bodies will be the next thing to waste away. To understand this more we have to talk about something called particle pollution. Particle pollution or more precisely, particulate matter or PM 2.5 [6], are the tiny solids or liquids that exist in the air. These harmful particles range from dust, dirt, soot, smoke and even drops of liquid that are in our air. One of the quickest ways to imagine this is simply by looking at the tailpipe of your car. You'll notice that

where the exhaust comes out it becomes completely dark-
ened by particulate matter. These toxins and chemical byproducts that end up in our atmosphere greatly affect our
health. According to the American Lung Association levels of
particle pollution above 30 parts per million are harmful to
human health.[7]

District 15, in Wilmington California, an outlying part of Los
Angeles, has some of the worst air quality in all of America.
Oil drilling here has been occurring since the 1800s and it's
taken a toll on the lives of these communities as the cause of
much suffering. The levels of particle pollution found in California's District 15 has been known to reach up to 100 parts
per million![8]

Levels of air toxins this high are a crime against humanity.

While everyone living in places where particle pollution levels are high is at risk, it is especially dangerous for the most
vulnerable among us. Studies have shown that at the top of
the list of those most affected are children. Children are
highly at risk to environmental changes and air quality due
"to their immature physiology and metabolism, their unique
exposure pathways, their biological sensitivities, and limits to
their adaptive capacity" - according to the U.S. Health and Climate Assessment.[9] Children also have a higher intake of air
relative to their body weight compared with adults. Children
exposed to poor air quality are faced with an array of adverse
health outcomes including asthma, a higher risk of infant

mortality rate, low-birth weight, childhood cancers, and neu-rodevelopmental effects such as autism, ADHD, and obesity.[10] Studies have also shown a direct link to air toxins and the dangers for pregnant mothers and their fetuses. In 2010 there were recorded 15,808 preterm births in the U.S. con-nected to exposure to particulate matter. Thirty-five percent of preterm births result in death. Given 15,808 preterm births resulting from particle pollution that's approximately 5,533 preventable infant deaths last year, almost double the number of people who died on 9/11/2001. In a recent larger study of over 32 million births, researchers found that there is a close association between bad birth outcomes and heat and air pollutants. Particulate matter, even in small amounts, causes 1 out of 9 premature births in the U.S. and 1 out of 6 for African Americans.[11]

Following children on the list of those most at risk are those with pre-existing conditions such as cardiovascular disease or diabetes, and then people of color. Recently, researchers have linked exposure to PM 2.5 with increased hospitaliza-tions for those with Alzheimer's disease and other demen-tias.[12] In 2015, an astronomical 9 million premature deaths were the result of diseases caused by air pollution, that is 16 percent of global deaths![13] [14] Nearly 5 in 10 people in the United States (approximately 45.8 percent of the population) live in counties that have unhealthy levels of air pollutants. Our waste is seeping into the very fabric of our planet. From the air we need to breathe, the water we need to drink, and the food we eat, each is being contaminated at rates never seen before. We now know that exposure to contaminated air, water, and soil kill more people than a high-sodium diet, obesity, alcohol, road accidents, or child and maternal malnutrition. These exposures produce three times as many deaths as AIDS, tuberculosis, and malaria combined, and nearly 15 times as many deaths as war and all forms of violence.[15] [16]

A study that tracked six U.S. cities from 1974 to 2009 suggested that cleaning up particle pollution had practically immediate health benefits. They estimated that the U.S. could prevent approximately 34,000 premature deaths a year if we could lower annual levels of particle pollution by 1 µg/m^3.[17][18] That is 1 microgram per cubic meter. To understand that quantity, imagine a tank the size of your washer and dryer combined. Then imagine taking ¼ teaspoon of sugar (which weighs about 1 gram) and dividing it into a million piles - that is a microgram! Now take one of these microscopic piles of sugar and dilute that into your big tank, that is 1 µg/m^3! [19]

Now what this tells us, is it only takes a very small amount of air pollution to have hazardous effects on human health. The research is clear, those who are being most affected today by air pollutants are the most vulnerable: our elderly, our children, and the unborn. How can we as the people of God take up our cross in love to change this?

What gives me hope here is that we know all "footprints" matter. If such tiny amounts can do so much damage in our world, surely you and I can begin making tiny differences in our lives that have the opposite effect. Quite literally, very little changes like...

Every time you turn off your car in the parking lot instead of letting it run.
Every time you turn your temperature to conserve energy in your home.
Every time you turn off that light.
Every time you choose to consume local goods.
Every time you eat beans instead of beef.
Each and every one of these actions are tiny ways of loving your neighbor that turn the needle just a little. Those little changes are big when you consider your impact, positive or negative, is the only thing you have to contribute.

Burning from the Flames

If you've ever stood alone on the beach looking out at the vastness of the ocean, you have probably known what it is to feel very small. This is the sentiment many express when it comes to humanity's ability to change the climate of our planet, as if it feels impossible because the world is just so... big. But if you've read this far, it is pretty easy to see how after years of never-ceasing crafting, consuming, and wasting of countless individuals... changing the surface of our world is exactly what we are doing. We have the "dominion" as Genesis frames it, and we can choose to do whatever we want with it, even to our own demise.

To get down to it, the amount of carbon and greenhouse gasses we are collectively putting into our atmosphere today is unprecedented, and it's warming the planet. Mitch Hescox president of the Evangelical Environmental Network, says it powerfully, "There is currently 40 percent more carbon into the atmosphere than God intended." Unfortunately, we're on track to make it much worse.

The Intergovernmental Panel on Climate Change (IPCC), with hundreds of scientists represented from countries all over the world, gave a special report in the fall of 2018 putting in perspective just how much we have altered our natural environment here on Earth. It is a grim report on how the world will be affected as we surpass a 1.5 degrees Celsius (2.7 degrees Fahrenheit) temperature increase.

But how much heat is that?
How badly can a couple of degrees really affect our planet?

To gain perspective, another unit of measurement that scientists use to study this are "joules." For those keeping score at home:

It takes one joule to lift an apple about three feet into the air.

It takes a 100-watt light bulb 1 second to use 100 joules.[20]

To put our situation into perspective, climate scientist Katherine Hayhoe points out that the amount of extra energy our planet has accumulated now adds up to more than 250 sextillion joules (that's 21 zeros if you're wanting to know) and counting! This number is currently climbing at a rate of four Hiroshima size bombs worth of energy per second![21] The conclusion? The Earth is running a tremendous fever and we must do something about it.

What could cause such a fever?

This warming isn't the result of natural outcomes or larger solar cycles. In fact, the Earth's temperature peaked about 8,000 years ago and has been on a steady decline toward what was going to be another ice age until around the Industrial Revolution began a couple of hundred years ago. Since then, Earth's temperature has been rising dramatically.[22]

If you were a gardener you wouldn't walk through your backyard, dig up all your plants, dump your trash where your garden was growing, and then decide to drive your car through it! Yet, as ridiculous as that sounds, it may very well be the most appropriate metaphor for what is now occurring in our global backyard. As a whole, we are essentially failing our role of stewardship of this great garden we call home. So much so, the planet is now severely sick.

Our atmosphere acts like a blanket around the planet. That blanket naturally holds heat (infrared radiation) coming to us from the sun while allowing a certain percentage to escape. For planet Earth historically this has been more like a summer throw blanket at the beach house; you might have some hot days, cool evenings, or a nice breeze, either way you're doing fine because your blanket is breathable. But now this blanket is becoming a heavy down-filled duvet, and we're beginning to sweat. What we're talking about is simple math at this point. The more greenhouse gas we are releasing into our atmosphere the heavier this blanket is becoming meanwhile less and less heat is escaping back into space, this is called the "greenhouse effect."

One of the deadliest contributors to this heating up is carbon dioxide (CO_2). Scientists use instruments and infrared light to measure the amounts of CO_2 that is in our atmosphere today, and currently the levels are higher than any of us have ever seen.[23] We can also measure how much of which kind of CO_2 is in the air (because there are multiple types). This is precisely what climate scientists have done and the results overwhelmingly point:

$\rightarrow$right back to **me**,
to **you**$\boxed{\searrow}$
$\boxed{\nearrow}$our **carbon**,
our **fuel**$\leftarrow$
our **coal**$\boxed{\checkmark}$
$\rightarrow$our **lifestyles**.

The greatest level of carbon dioxide blanketing our atmosphere today is anthropogenic emissions, that is human-generated CO_2. We can measure and see that the fingerprint of the majority of CO_2 in the atmosphere is from burning fossil fuels, not from natural causes (such as erupting volcanoes or simply us breathing). We can tell this because human-generated carbon dioxide has a different number of isotopes than naturally occurring carbon dioxide. From 1,000 to a couple of hundred years ago the amount of carbon in our atmosphere was fairly static. But since that time the amount of CO_2 being put into our atmosphere has spiked tremendously.[24] [25] Now in the last couple of decades, it feels as if we are climbing this gas-induced heat summit. In fact, 9 out of the 10 warmest years on record have occurred just since 2005.

While the science is clear, it isn't simply reading data that tells us how our planet and ecosystems are changing. Around the globe, there are more than 26,500 indicators that the planet is warming.[26]

Some of these indicators you might already know or have noticed without connecting it back to climate change. Sea levels are rising as arctic sea ice is melting away, coral reefs are disappearing, increasing wildfires and extreme weather events, the cherry trees are blossoming earlier, and migratory birds move further north each year. It doesn't take a scientist graphing carbon isotopes to see these changes, just someone with a willingness to observe.[27]

For decades now the ocean has functioned as a giant heat absorber. The sea has quite literally been "taking the heat" for us. Now as the oceans are warming to higher and higher temperatures it will begin affecting all forms of life.

Even though our feet are planted on the ground, our lives are bound with the health of the ocean. Water is beginning to evaporate, creating larger, more fierce and frequent storm systems. In the coming years we will witness floods of new magnitudes, the evacuations of coastal lands and great migrations of refugees like never before. Poor communities will be affected the most (as they are without a voice in what happens to them) and millions will be forced to flee their homes. In other areas of the world we will continue to see droughts like the major one already witnessed from 2011 to 2015 in California, which was the driest period since record keeping began. [28]

For us reading this tucked away in our air-conditioned homes it may be difficult to see, but the death toll from increasing global heat is on the rise. It isn't just from heat stroke and related conditions, but from respiratory disease, cardiovascular disease, and cerebrovascular diseases as well. These heat waves are associated with increased hospital admissions for respiratory, cardiovascular, and kidney disorders. From 1998 to 2015 more than 166,000 people died because of heatwaves. That includes 70,000 people who died due to the extreme heatwave in Europe in 2003. In fact, that was just Europe's inaugural heatwave, as they've now had five "500-year summers" in the last 15 years![29] And here in the United States places such as St. Louis, Philadelphia, Chicago, and Cincinnati have experienced a dramatic increase in death tolls during heat waves as well. [30] [31]

One expected but often unmentioned result of all these changes in our environment is mass-migration. In the Pacific Islands the sea level is rising at a rate of 12 millimeters per year with a conservative global estimated reach of over 3 feet by the year 2100. This may not sound like a lot yet, but in the western Pacific eight islands have already been submerged and two more are about to follow prompting large-scale migration.

Leitu Frank, a 32-year-old resident of the island of Tuvalu in the British Commonwealth reflects on her homeland, "Before, the sand used to stretch out far, and when we swam, we could see the seafloor, and the coral. Now, it is cloudy all the time, and the coral is dead. Tuvalu is sinking."[32] [33] [34]

In 2017 the world saw somewhere between 22 and 24 million people migrating from their homes due to sudden onset weather events such as flooding, intensified storms, fires, and droughts. The World Bank has estimated that by 2050 we will see 143 million more climate migrants from Latin America, sub-Saharan Africa, and Southeast Asia.[35] [36]

As the deterioration of our climate continues, mass-migrations won't be the only result, but through symptoms like desertification, loss of biodiversity, ocean acidification, shifting rain patterns, and sea-level rise we will see an unprecedented influx of humanitarian crises as well.

If our reliance on fossil fuels and nonrenewable resources continues at current consumption rates, then as a species we will face a huge existential crisis in our lifetime. A ninety-seven percent consensus of climate scientists confirm that there is human-caused climate change happening and that we must evacuate our utter dependence on fossil fuels quickly. If we cannot greatly change our consumption habits and industrial practices enough to reduce our carbon emissions by 45% by the year 2030 and reaching net-zero by 2050, it could be catastrophic. Warming our planet 1.5°C or higher greatly increases the risk of irreversible changes and even the collapse of ecosystems. Our food supply, our water sources, our economy, our health, and our future are all interconnected with the choices that you and I will make today. [37]

I don't know about you, but I believe this all sounds quite a bit outside of what God had in mind when he created this place and called it *tov.*

I don't know about you, but it seems to me that our vocation of serving and keeping this sacred garden has been not just neglected, but abused.

I don't know about you, but if there is a way to make all this right again, I want to be a part of that.

A sustainable and regenerative world is possible, but there is no time to waste.

Respond & Reflect

I still remember the night, sitting on the couch, and truly absorbing this information about how our planet is undergoing such change. I sat reading reports, reviews, and data on the projected consequences of our over-consumption. It was, and still can be, very overwhelming. Sometimes before we can be moved to hopeful action, we must come toe to toe with the dark reality of our situation.

Respond → *Do your own research.*

Go to: nca2018.globalchange.gov to see the Fourth National Climate Assessment. Click on "Chapters" to read about the area you live in and the impacts of how climate is changing.

Watch: Go to Youtube.com and type in "What is God's Creation Telling Us? Climate Science 101" to hear Climate Scientist, Katharine Hayhoe explain how our climate is changing.

Respond → *One of the quickest actions you can take to heal our planet is, inaction.*

Try to take 5 fewer car trips this week! Really challenge yourself about the necessity of all that you are doing in the world. When it comes to emitting carbon, one of the very worst choices you can make is taking a flight somewhere. Could you reduce your harmful impact on the world by not flying unless absolutely essential?

Meanwhile, the best thing that you can be *doing* is to plant a tree! To this day, there is no better action or technology that does more good towards climate justice than God's gift of a tree!

Respond → Explore Project Drawdown - The world's most comprehensive resource for climate solutions: Drawdown.org

Reflect → How did this chapter sit with you?

If we're honest, talking about how our climate is changing can be riddled with politics. Sometimes, certain people or certain ideas become associated with this subject making it difficult to hear with fresh ears and see with untarnished eyes. You can be sure though, that caring for God's creation is not affiliated with any political party, but with our calling as a people of the kingdom of heaven.

Is this information challenging for you to hear? Share your struggles.

What information in this chapter comes as most of a surprise to you?

Where are some places, or what are some ways in which you've witnessed the environment changing in the last several years? How about more recently? This could be observations from your backyard or something you've seen in the news.

Maybe what is most appropriate after learning about the state of our hurting planet is taking some time to grieve. Take some time, allowing yourself to mourn. We must mourn.
We must hear these cries and cry ourselves.
We must allow ourselves to be moved by the great sadness of the degradation of this beautiful planet that we've so taken for granted.
Take a moment to share or journal what saddens you the most about the current state of our home?

We are now God's steward. We are indebted to him for all we have…. A steward is not at liberty to use what is lodged in his hands as he pleases, but as his master pleases…
- John Wesley [38]

Tiny House

Working bi-vocational as a pastor trash hauler can get exhausting! So we've attempted a number of creative methods to gain a bit of income over the years. My wife, the kids, and I live in a small home from the '50s that has a little weird laundry mudroom off to the side. For years this room simply acted as a catch-all. It was full of books, bikes, a water heater, a washer, and anything else we needed to hide! Some time ago now my wife, who is gifted with the endless churn of brilliant ideas, looked at me and said, "You know we should turn that mudroom into a tiny house and rent it out!" God bless her, like most of her crazy ideas I laughed at it. Then of course we did it. It took us the better part of a year, lots of hard work, and more love than we deserve from some close friends, but it happened! Now attached to the side of our house, you can walk through a pergola into the front door of a 165 square foot tiny house. It's complete with a full bathroom (tub and shower), kitchen, and a loft bed! Still most days I literally can't believe we finished that project. Not only did we do it, but the majority of the remodel we were able to accomplish with reclaimed materials!

From the pergola to all the doors, windows, sink, toilet, tile, bed, stools, cabinets, swing, toaster oven and so on we salvaged as used items from other places and people. It's astonishing how much we don't ever need to buy new. We enjoy sharing this information with all who stay here because it is a testament to how truly doable reclaimed living is, and how good it can look!

The other part I find fascinating is that we Airbnb the space and it is booked pretty much every night. So many people are fascinated with tiny living. This obviously is nothing new if you've seen any of the dozens of shows out there about tiny homes. Our space simply gives folks the opportunity to try it on for a night or two. The funny thing, when you get to thinking about it, is how most everyone lived in small little houses once upon a time in history. Now our imaginations crave to know if that is *really* something we could pull off today.

Could we do without all these *things?*
Could we live without so much?
Do you ever stop to ponder what exactly our homes are full of? I've cleaned out many homes over the years, full of so many items left behind. These aren't evictions, these are just homes full of items no-one bothered moving... because at some point "stuff" so abounds it just isn't that special. Odds are that you have a home full of items you hardly use or look at but continue to keep these things because "just in case" or they are some-how sentimental for you... or you're just hoarding!

Funny enough there are almost always certain items that will be left behind at any given property...

Basketball goal
Grill
Sandbox
Anything in the shed!
Exercise equipment
Old Tires
Anything in the attic or crawlspace!

I don't think it's any surprise that in a culture overwhelmed with so many things, there is a rising group of people not only interested but absolutely craving...
Simplicity
Minimalism
Modesty of stuff
Just the essentials
A life of less!

We now live in a time when we are inundated with not only an overabundance of materiality but also information. Is there any coincidence that there would be a rise in depression and anxiety rates along with a rise in information accessibility? It's all just too much. How might we even lessen our habits of consuming information? Can we simplify the space around us and learn the practice of simplicity of media?

There is a wasting that happens in our lives when our days become a fight through mounds of media and belongings. Perhaps the advantage of being poor is that you have fewer decisions to make. Fewer options all the way around. Choices about what to wear or what to eat or how far you can go today are all very limited. I believe Jesus knew the freedom of this very well. Why are the gospels always holding up the poor as those with quick access into the kingdom of heaven? There is simply not as much in the way... literally! Yet, there is also a childlikeness to poverty. In that, we are positioned as the receivers in society more than the givers. Too many of us only view ourselves as the givers and never the receivers.

Yet, naturally, those in such positions do everything they can to "escape" their humble post, and ironically those distanced from such a life seek a kingdom that can only be found through it.

I've often thought that the greatest challenge for a pastor must be pastoring a church in the suburbs of America. Could there be a more challenging place for the gospel to take root than the very seat of American comfort? When there is lack of need, when you have nothing you can offer anyone, when everyone already has everything, the gospel is forced into intangible spaces. When there is the lack of the lack, we miss what this life is all about. Because it is *through* our lack that God always...
Moves
Creates
Appears
Resurrects
Redeems
And is born!

This is the reason most wealthy places frequently transform the gospel of Christ into an intangible message about a heaven somewhere else. Because we simply cannot reconcile Jesus' gospel with a lifestyle of overconsumption and wasteful comfort. Faced with the choice of becoming less, becoming more reliant on our community, saving less to love more, *or* altering the message to keep our cozy lifestyle intact... the latter is an easy choice.

Still though, there is an unmistakable stirring of the western heart that is desiring for more. Because frankly, you can only do so much of the American dream before you realize it's more like a nightmare... an unquenchable thirst in a land of dirty water and a starvation amidst desertification.

The question surfacing around us today asks ...

could there be more with less?

CHAPTER SIX

Opening the Consuming Eye

He also said, "With what can we compare the kingdom of God, or what parable will we use for it? It is like a mustard seed, which, when sown upon the ground, is the smallest of all the seeds on Earth; yet when it is sown it grows up and becomes the greatest of all shrubs, and puts forth large branches, so that the birds of the air can make nests in its shade."

Mark 4:30-32

I love seeds. Seeds are fascinating. From such an infinitesimal element can come perpetual life. Just imagine one little bell pepper seed that gets planted. It produces dozens of peppers in one season. In just one of those dozens of peppers are dozens of seeds, each one capable of producing its own set of peppers! On and on and on! It's no wonder Jesus clung to the image of the seed to talk about the kingdom of heaven over and over. It's beautiful, it's everywhere, it's prolific, and it's itty bitty with gargantuan potential.

Could living into becoming a citizen of the kingdom of God have something to do with becoming as small as a seed? Could something about our living-little hold the secret to providing life for all?
Might our meekness precede our inheritance of the Earth?

Would Jesus really call us to live little meager lives?

If so, could you do it?

Perfection and Possession

The young man said to him, "I have kept all these; what do I still lack?" Jesus said to him, "If you wish to be perfect, go, sell your possessions, and give the money to the poor, and you will have treasure in heaven; then come, follow me." When the young man heard this word, he went away grieving, for he had many possessions. Then Jesus said to his disciples, "Truly I tell you, it will be hard for a rich person to enter the kingdom of heaven. Again I tell you, it is easier for a camel to go through the eye of a needle than for someone who is rich to enter the kingdom of God."
- Matthew 19:20-22

In Matthew 19 Jesus invites this wealthy young man into a smaller existence. We often read this passage as if it's only about the young man's life. Yet, a closer read reveals two truths. There is good news for the poor that occurs as this man sells his possessions, but not only that, it is good for this man to become poorer himself. Jesus invites us into a kingdom that lifts up those in poverty and brings low those who have hoarded wealth.

But Jesus in the Gospels isn't the first place we hear of something like this. No, all the way back in the Pentateuch we learn about God's plan for his people and their possessions and land. It was called the year of Jubilee. You've probably heard of it. It pretty much has fairytale status. Mainly because as far as recorded history informs us, it never happened. [1]

The idea was that every 50 years you got everything back. If you were a slave, you were released. If you had debts, they were forgiven. If you lost your land it was returned. Pretty epic, right? Yeah, it would have been! But as we all know, when you get to dealing with people's money, debts, land, and freedom... well that gets pretty political. And when it comes to forgiving loans and forgoing power, those in power never seem to go for it for some reason!

Since the start, God has been against systemic poverty and against hoarding wealth. The kingdom of heaven it would seem works toward everyone having what they need, equally. Which inevitably was the thing about the early church in Acts that we all love to quote and are attracted to!

But what do we do today when our camels are bigger than ever? When here in America 5 percent of the population own two-thirds of the wealth?[2] As long as we see bigger as better can we ever truly follow the One who calls us to shed our excess in order to enter the kingdom?

The Miracle of Smallness

Bigger is better! That's at least what most of us have always heard, right? We strive for bigger opportunities, larger homes, bigger and better jobs and incomes. We pray for our churches to increase in size. We pray for our businesses to grow. We pray for our investments to grow. We pray for large-scale success. It's never enough to sell our product locally, we've got to get on Shark Tank! Because bigger just seems better, right? It's the idea that the more we grow, accumulate, produce, advance, expand, increase the better off our business, our home, or our lives will be.

The more I read our gospels the more difficult this idea of bigger-better becomes for me. It seems that from the very birth of our Savior to the way he died, and even what we know about his resurrection appearances, it's all very small. Even as Jesus spread the good news it was with a few faithful disciples proclaiming words such as...

Blessed are the poor
Blessed are the meek
Blessed is this widow who gave all she had
Faith like a mustard seed
The kingdom of heaven is like yeast... (by the way have you ever held a single fragment of yeast in your hand?)

Jesus moved about to one village, one miracle, one meal, one healing, one person at a time. One moment that strikes me from Mark 1 when Jesus has been teaching and healing many people in Capernaum. It said that the "whole city" had been at the door of the little house where Jesus stayed. The next morning Jesus went out to pray, and in a typical panic, the disciples woke up and were looking for him (For some reason

Jesus never just leaves a sticky note... "Gone out to pray BRB!"). Back at the house, there's likely still some overnight campers waiting for their healing. When they finally find Jesus and inform him that "everyone is searching for you!" Jesus responds with, "Let us go on..."

Let us go on. Really? Jesus that's what you want to do? There are folks crawling through the windows needing healing here in Capernaum... and you want to keep moving?

What's intriguing is although there is still so much good to do where he is at... he decides to keep moving. The model Jesus leaves us of proclaiming the good news isn't a model where one person goes and does all the good there is to do.

Jesus doesn't heal everyone.
Jesus doesn't get everywhere.
Jesus himself doesn't do all the good.
Jesus is on the move.

Jesus is making disciples. The model left for us by Christ walking on Earth is one of discipleship. The places he doesn't go he leaves in the hands and care of his disciples. The model Jesus leaves for us is human. It has boundaries. It is located in a certain part of the world. It is small.

Jesus didn't get very far in his life. He never traveled around the world. Jesus didn't have a passport. Jesus didn't have a big house (or a mortgage at all). Jesus didn't have a big life, at least in the ways we would label "big" today. Jesus led a small kingdom of God oriented life.

The miraculous-ness of all that happened in Jesus' life was the result of what happens when someone's life is lived in a simple kingdom way. That is the miracle of smallness. Jesus never said, "we're going to need a bigger temple here!" Actually, what Jesus said is, "see that temple, it's coming down!" Jesus' life was (and still is) an embodiment of the infiltration of small kingdom ways of living. It is in living in this small, simple, steadfast way that the miracles of the kingdom of God thrive. It is the soil in which springs to life the abundance of heaven on Earth. That is how a little holy yeast slowly works its way through the whole batch of dough and how tiny little pepper seeds create all the peppers of the future.

Bigger, Better, Bootstrap (Backward) Gospel

But those who want to be rich fall into temptation and are trapped by many senseless and harmful desires that plunge people into ruin and destruction. For the love of money is a root of all kinds of evil, and in their eagerness to be rich some have wandered away from the faith and pierced themselves with many pains. But as for you, man of God, shun all this; pursue righteousness, godliness, faith, love, endurance, gentleness.
- 1 Timothy 6:9-11

It is no coincidence that a culture that readily promotes and rewards a lifestyle of pulling ourselves up by our bootstraps and climbing corporate ladders has delivered a bigger-better translation of the gospels. We had to have a different narrative if we were to keep our castles and our large investments alongside our worship services and scripture readings. If we are to keep living like the Babylonians rather than the Israelites, we would have to tweak the narrative. We would need to adjust the lens through which we read the gospels.

Ironically, being the trash man puts you toe to toe with some really wealthy folks sometimes. That is because the owners and investors of these large, beautiful homes that emerge all over the city are the ones calling to get all the not-so-beautiful things removed. For some, the script seems to hold true that those who work long hard hours day in and day out are the ones succeeding at the bigger-better game. (Although many work the same long hard hours and are unable to climb the bigger-better ladder because of decades of systemic oppression.) Yet, those I've witnessed who are the most "successful" at a bigger-better life are always busy making, feeding, fueling the machine so that the wheels keep turning without ceasing. The bigger-better lifestyle is in fact trapped by the demands of its own existence.

Sometimes when you are so wrapped up in your own "progress", nose to the grindstone, you never look up long enough to realize that you're not getting anywhere. And what is worse, you're even missing everything important and special about your life.

I wonder if sometimes, deep down, we already know this.

But once you've been in the cycle for this long, how do you get out? To admit you've done it wrong all this time would be facing your greatest fears. It would be like death.

Bigger-better progress in the world always demands more energy and more blood than you were actually wanting to give in the first place. It demands more than you were created to give. But we often give it anyway. Because once you're in this cycle... it's all too easy to get stuck and almost impossible it seems to get out. At least that's what Jesus told the "rich young ruler" as we like to call him. The man walks away from Jesus downcast because he has great wealth. Once things get this big in life all the cogs are working together to keep the machine going, right?

The employees must get paid.
The equipment must be maintained.
We've got to insure all this *and* everyone.
It costs a lot of money to heat and cool this place.
City codes say we must have a bathroom here.
And of course we have to keep all this oiled and fueled up.
The engine demands it.

Bigger-better looks something like this ...

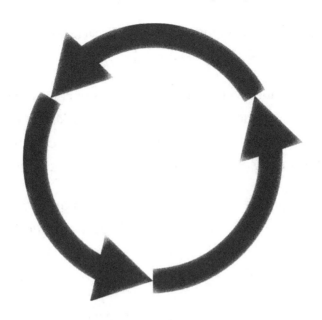

At first glance it looks like a blurred recycling symbol. Until you realize that it isn't a recycling symbol at all. The motion is in fact moving in the wrong direction. It is rotating in reverse. Also, there is no curving round, each arrow is un-transformed as it simply moves, pushing what it has to the next arrow in false hopes of becoming something more.

This is the harmful cycle of a system of taking, making, consuming, and wasting.

It is a shadow of a life well-lived. It is an illusion of growth. What it produces simply goes on to fuel up the next arrow in an endless hamster wheel of a ghostly existence. It transforms nothing, it resurrects nothing, it simply exists with the endless goal of becoming bigger-better. It is the illusion of having more. Those trapped in this purgatory become willing participants in this shadowy broken life cycle. This sort of living moves us and society backward.

Many speak about our current economic structure in the world as being linear. The reason is that we take from the Earth, we make whatever it is that we want, we consume it, and then we discard it. We do all this in the name of growth.

In 2015 a study revealed that a shocking two-thirds of the 102 billion tons of minerals, ore, fossil fuels, and biomass we took from the planet was wasted, either emitted as carbon or lost to the landfills.[3]

I would suggest that this broken system isn't linear but is actually moving backward. We are "running Genesis in reverse," as author, activist and United Methodist layman Bill Mckibben would say.[4] [5]There is no neutral position left for us today, we are either being co-creators with God as regenerative forces in the world, or are participating in the de-creation, the unraveling, and undoing of the very place we were designed to take care of. Mountaintops are being removed, forests burned, ancient jungles excavated, and historic coral reefs bleached away. The difficult truth is that we are either actively moving toward a different sort of lifestyle that doesn't participate in these realities or are left to simply go with the decimating flow.

The more we adhere to this backward system that we've created, the more creation will waste away. The longer we assume that living bigger is living better, we will continue to strain our planet from being "tov" as well.

A New Ark

Now the Earth was corrupt in God's sight, and the Earth was filled with violence. And God saw that the Earth was corrupt; for all flesh had corrupted its ways upon the Earth.

But I will establish my covenant with you; and you shall come into the ark, you, your sons, your wife, and your son's wives with you. And of every living thing...
- **Genesis 6:11-12; 18-19**

The story of Noah and his family serves as a warning and an emblem of hope for us today. In the wake of "running Genesis in reverse" and the current corruption of our planet, might we be called to build a new ark, a refuge for God's work in the world? Might God be calling out to the few faithful to respond in ways never before seen? Might our God still be calling us into audacious and regenerative construction in order to rescue creation?

Noah and his family would have been the village lunatics of their time. A flood that was going to cover the entire Earth? No way. A giant boat? Whoever heard of such?

The funny thing about reading these ancient Biblical stories is how quick we are to place ourselves as the good central figure. Are we Noah here? Are we the righteous faithful ones hearing the voice of God even though it sounds different than every other voice around us?

Or are we the ones not heeding the warning? Are we the community who calls Noah crazy? Are we the ones unwilling to acknowledge the observable rain clouds and opt into ark building and creation saving action?

In 2018 a study was published in the Proceedings of the National Academy of Sciences that gave an updated census of Earth's biomass.[6] We discovered that humans and our livestock (cows, chickens, pigs, etc.) comprise close to 96% of all mammals on the planet. This means that dolphins, bears, lions, badgers, foxes, moose, sea-lions, wolves, elephants, whales, giraffes (... you get the point) now only comprise a total of 4% of the mammals left on Earth! This is devastating information. Humans, who account for only 0.01 percent of all biomass on the planet, are playing an oppressive role over creation (especially in the ways that we eat). How ironic that the creature that God creates at the very end of the 6th day of creation, the one who is designed to be a creative life-giving participant with God, becomes the one to later unravel the previous 6 days of creation?

Are we the faithful Noah, hearing the call of God to protectively care for creation? Or are we the community who calls Noah a crazy, tree-hugging hippie?

In which of these camps are we?

The story of Noah's ark is about how the faithful people of God engage with God in a history altering salvific plan that involves rescuing every species on Earth in the face of cataclysmic extinction. Today, we now know that we are facing the Earth's 6th mass extinction. [7]

How may we learn from this story, may we hear the warnings, and participate in the crafting of new arks in our world today, while there is still time?

I can't help but wonder, are we unfaithful Noahs?

The Consumer Eye

You have already spent enough time in doing what the Gentiles like to do, living in licentiousness, passions, drunkenness, revels, carousing, and lawless idolatry. They are surprised that you no longer join them in the same excesses of dissipation, and so they blaspheme. But they will have to give an accounting to him who stands ready to judge the living and the dead. For this is the reason the gospel was proclaimed even to the dead, so that, though they had been judged in the flesh as everyone is judged, they might live in the spirit as God does.
- 1 Peter 4:3-6

The excesses of dissipation. Doesn't sin always seem to involve some form of excess? Peter warns the church against this culture of an abundance of dissolute living. Yet it seems that no matter how many times the Scripture cautions us against this excessive way of living, the gods of gain are always on standby to whisper deceiving words into our ears. The idols of consumption are ready to grab our attention.

Thank the Lord that the Spirit of God is able to set us free even from the snares of sin we've willingly entered... if we will repent and turn away.

A couple of Christmas seasons ago Emily and I took a trip to Memphis to spend the entire day walking around a giant no-window fluorescent-lit shrine of compressed cardboard and Swedish meatballs... called IKEA. As we snaked our way through the maze of bedroom suits and model kitchens I turned to Emily and said, *"This is like a prayer labyrinth for consumerism."* If you've ever been, you know what I'm talking about!

There's just something tempting about those sleek designs, those European delectables, and those perfect organization solutions! It makes you want a second home just so that you can fill it with stuff again!

To be honest, perhaps we all need to spend a little time confessing the ways we've been paying homage to the gods of consumerism. Who hasn't spent a little time in these

labyrinths and at these altars? Who hasn't at some point sac-
rificed to the gods made of rose gold?

One of the joys of parenting is getting to teach your children
how the world operates. As parents we have the first opportunities to frame the minds of our children. All they know is
what you teach them… until they make friends of course! I
love teaching our children about our connection to the Earth,
the water, the soil, and our place in it all. One of the fun conversations is always about where stuff comes from. Our food,
our clothing, our toys, our furniture all has an origin story
and an end-of-life story. Inevitably this conversation arises
out of need as all the lights in the house are left on… Or water
is left running for what seems like forever… Or a devastating
amount of toilet paper ends up clogging the toilet! You know,
regular moments of chaos with kids…

Sweetie, did you know that this right here is made from trees?

Whaaaaat? *insert huge eyes here*

Yeah, they have to cut down trees to make this. Crazy, right?

Oh my word… *she looks out the window*

*They cut up the wood in factories, drive it around the country
in big trucks, put it on shelves in the store, and we buy it.*

I want to go to the store!

Me continuing the lesson *But what happens is, eventually it gets so used or old that we have to get rid of it...*

there's a gasp and tears come because my precious daughter can't get rid of anything

And then we have to buy a new one.

Yay!

In a nutshell (literally!), this is how the whole machine works.

One continual outpouring and draining of consumption and waste.

The world of marketing has got us by the power cord! If there is something you're interested in purchasing, the algorithms will be adding that item to your online cart before the day is done! Just as one afternoon I spent a few minutes searching online for used hiking shoes and the next minute I was receiving Facebook ads for outdoor boots. As it happens, now a year later I'm still getting shoe ads! Is there really any escape from it all in our day, short of taking our monastic vows and moving to the Abbey?

Hours out of each day we fixate on the screen, the billboard, the commercial and with each one a whisper of desire is planted in our psyche about the next thing we want. Social media is the next and deadliest wave of consumeristic psychological onslaught. Artificial intelligence (AI) algorithms know what we want even more than we do ourselves and they keep us hooked for one reason; to sell to us. Then by the time Black Friday comes along each year it's as if the Earth is groaning and raging against the machine. (By the way, it's called "Black Friday" because many large companies are "in the red" until the holidays come around.) This posture of possession is consuming the Earth whole with each new item that we must have. Every new phone that comes out, gaming system, fad, trinket, style, new car, and so on. Every time we remodel, get a new appliance, or go to the dangerous land of IKEA, we are participating in a continual flow of purchasing and trashing.

No doubt, living life does involve stuff! Consumption is necessary to stay alive!

Although consumption is not evil, over-consumption, consuming cheap goods, and consuming in a selfish and harmful posture are all ways our consumption gets entangled with sin. This is especially true as consumption becomes an act of idol worship for us.

We are a society that loves things. Things make up our lives. Every day we make that online order, we run that errand, because we are in search of the next right item to improve our lives. Yes, of course, there are most definitely essentials that we need, but for the most part so much of what we "need" — we don't need.

Shopping and consuming can be an addiction — even a form of recreation. There are entire YouTube channels dedicated to watching other people shop and open boxes and gifts! Ultimately, there is something addictive about the process of it all, the going out, the unwrapping, the newness, the smell of fresh sneakers, the swiping of the card... it releases the pleasure endorphins inside us. Honestly, the item itself is often just... whatever! It's given away, disposed of after a bit, or upgraded. Because what really drives us is the feeling of making the purchase, getting the upgrade, surrendering to the splurge.[8]

We must turn away from our urges toward consumption for consumption-sake and begin to take stock of each and every thing we decide to buy. How might you challenge yourself to a shopping fast? Could you do a "Whole30" for stuff consumption? Often if we can allow ourselves to be "hungry" for a moment we can see with more clarity how much something really means to us.

Moving forward requires a new clarity in the way we see everything.

We must put on a new set of lenses. Or in other words, open another eye.

What if we had a third eye (as the mystics say) for all that we come in contact with? What if we could see even our trash at new depths being intertwined with the forests, the oceans, our soil, our sisters and brothers, and us? What if we could see beyond the cost of an item and the usefulness of it, to see the *Earth-price* of every item we consider consuming? What is the environmental cost of this purchase and how does this affect my brothers and sisters in the world? Just like the conversation with my daughter, could we start to see behind the usefulness, desire and financial cost? Is it possible to begin to see the reflections of heaven and hell in the traces of packaging we leave behind?

Already Everything

Then the father said to him, 'Son, you are always with me, and all that is mine is yours.
- **Luke 15:31**

How much is enough? How do we know? When do we stop? The issues of consumption and waste go hand in hand with confronting our beliefs about enough. Enough for some people seems to be lacking for others. Yet, the lack of one might just be wealth for someone else. So, what exactly is enough?

What if many of these complications around waste are derived from our belief that we don't have enough? It is the desire for more that generates this pattern of purchase and waste. Consuming more than we actually need is a wide web that catches many. The strands of this web are,

The mindset of scarcity and the fear of there not being
enough,
The coalescence of our happiness with our belongings,
The deep neural pathways of spending money,
The addictive habit of attaining new possessions,
The lure of keeping up with the times,
The cultural game of bigger-better,
And of course, there's always just plain old greed.

We are often quick to denounce such hedonistic devotion to
the gods of consumerism. But a sober look into our own lives
and homes and modes of transportation will quickly reveal
that most of us are still playing some part of the game and
getting caught in the web.

Perhaps step one is confessing our shortcomings here and
owning the truth of it. We are a bit stuck in a system that
pushes, drives and thrusts these material goods upon us.
Meanwhile, it continually feeds us a myth that says, *"If you
stop, you'll die. If you cease to consume this way, the world
will crumble."* It becomes this marriage of our fears and
our insatiable desires that makes this web so deadly. As
long as we are afraid and hungry for more, we will continue to keep corrupt and broken businesses in the black.
Except the catch is now we are trapped here in the web
ourselves.

The gospel has always been about receiving our daily bread, about having enough for today. Jesus teaches us to pray a prayer that asks not for extravagance, wealth, or plenty but simply enough for this day right here. Faith is walking with God day by day, not getting lost in tomorrow and the needs therein, but believing that we have enough breath and life for this moment.

I wonder though if actually it's never been about even *having enough* but rather *being enough?* Through Jesus Christ, once we receive that we are already enough, that we are already good, that we are already here *with* God, then we won't exert so much of our energy, time, and resources on that next purchase or "good" to make us good. When everything is already yours what more could you want? Is this not what Jesus is trying to continually give us with his Spirit, the knowledge of enough?

But like the other son in Jesus' parable about "The prodigal son" - we become so upset and focused on the wrong things. The older son becomes so upset that his younger brother receives such an extravagant party and grandiose meal that he can't receive what he already has.

"But he answered his father, 'Listen! For all these years I have been working like a slave for you, and I have never disobeyed your command; yet you have never given me even a young goat so that I might celebrate with my friends. But when this son of yours came back, who has devoured your property

with prostitutes, you killed the fatted calf for him!'
Then the father said to him, 'Son, you are always with me, and
all that is mine is yours." [9]

Is it possible to be blinded by our own sense of what justice is?
Might we be unable to give up our consumerist ways as a society because it all just doesn't sound fair?

Does true forgiveness ever crawl under your skin?

Parenting our two little girls we spend a great deal of time
and energy wrestling around with the idea of fairness. Children want to know how the world works and seem to come
to us already wired for this notion of things being fair.
"I want what she has."
"Why do they have that, but we don't?"
"She's not sharing!"
Parenting sometimes feels like refereeing a soccer game
where there's no scoreboard and no shin guards!

Ultimately, I believe children are on to something important
as they are learning to express this idea of justice through
fairness. But there are two primary postures that you can
have with fairness (and with all things):

You can be selflessly fair, or selfishly fair.

One of these postures declares there is enough to go around,
and the other perpetuates the cycle of waste.

One of the ironies of growing up has been discovering just how much adults still spend all their time talking about fairness. But it is the same sort of fairness most children are arguing about, a tit for tat fairness. Somehow thousands of years have gone by, and our systems of justice have hardly evolved past being an "eye for an eye." We say, "I'll get you because you got me!"

Jesus confronts our old ideals of justice by transforming our narrative. He tells us to love our neighbors and our enemies.[10] Jesus understood that salvation is always collective. Your life will always be related to the life of your neighbor. Even if you choose to withdraw yourself from community, that community is now lacking because of your self-removal. The reason for this is that humanity is *collectively created in the image of a Triune God.* "Let us make humankind in our image," God says on that 6th day of creation.[11] God is communal and so are we.

It shouldn't come as a shock that in order to solve our planetary crisis of a posture of wastefulness we must return to the knowledge of humanity as a collective. Our consumerist culture attempts to make each person believe that we are alone, that "you are a person who must work your own way to the top, making it on your own, achieving your own American dream no matter who or what stands in your way." This kind of thinking will always lend itself to the belief that life is a battle to be won over another, rather than a beautiful collaborative garden to grow.

Thankfully the father in this parable still finds all his children and says, "You are always with me, and everything I have is yours."

The question is, can you see that? Can you receive that? Can you live like you believe that?

This book is about the "unseen world of waste..." – because ultimately before we change anything about our own actions in the world, whether that's about our trash or our consumption, we always first must adjust the way that we see.

Salvation always begins with the gift of sight.

In these pages we are spending a great deal of time trying to see the waste that isn't typically seen. Everything from a floating garbage patch to the warming blanket of CO_2 in our atmosphere, to landfills, to the pollutants in our water and soil, and so on.

But seeing the unseen isn't simply about the physical elements tossed away in our world. No, the deeper thing that we must address is the actual WAY in which we see. In other words, what is it inside of us that makes us act the way that we do? What is it inside of us that causes us to manufacture such waste and disparity in the world?

What would it mean for us to address what is inside our hearts that causes us to see one way or another?

Because there is a certain way of seeing that harms our neighbor, that oppresses, that is destructive and wasteful, that is greedy and lustful, that is unloving.

And there is another way of seeing that is selfless, healing, mending, holy, and loving.

Only by first addressing our own sight in the world will we be able to care for the planet, the poor, and mend that great chasm of brokenness.

Respond & Reflect

Respond → *Assess your footprint!*

Visit **FootPrintNetwork.org** and see what your ecological footprint is and ways to respond.

Respond → *Ark of Taste*

Visit **Slowfoodusa.org/ark-of-taste** and learn about how eating endangered species can actually save them from extinction!

Reflect → Out of the Scriptures mentioned in this chapter, which one stood out to you the most?

How is Scripture lighting up for you in new ways around our resources and consumption?

What are ways that you see cultural values in conflict with the kingdom of God when it comes to issues of economics?

How does this idea of running Genesis in reverse connect with you? Is it possible that we could be de-creating?

What are some ways that you've stored up treasures on Earth that God might be asking you to part with?

Do you feel challenged by the idea of living smaller?

The "Gift" of Christmas

Have you ever noticed the cans of waste awaiting pick up on the first trash day after Christmas! Each December our landfills are overrun through the celebration of the birth of our Lord. How does any of this make sense? (By the way, buying each other new toys may not be the most appropriate way to celebrate the birth of God Incarnate... somebody had to say it! Feel free to call me the Grinch!)

Since the birth of our girls Emily and I decided that we weren't going to celebrate Christmas with a bunch of presents. Of course, this was highly problematic at first with gloating grandparents! But ultimately this "rule" gives way to deeper and richer interactions with one another over the holidays. We dig deeper into Advent and then celebrate all 12 days of Christmas with the children, doing something special each day. Sometimes this may involve a creative gift or two that helps us better engage together as a family, but for the most part it is oriented around shared experiences. It's a bit of work but it becomes more beautiful each year as we find our own traditions of reflecting on the story of Jesus, spending time together, and serving over the days of Christmas.

A couple of years ago on the 11th day of Christmas, our kids unwrapped a box to discover a first-generation 1985 Nintendo. It was so much fun! Mario and Luigi, Duck Hunt, and little controllers with two red buttons! This was my sister's and mine when we were kids and now watching our girls getting to play with this game is amazing.

Naturally, they had no idea what it was, but our kids wouldn't know an XBOX if they saw one either. A 30-year-old Nintendo is a hit with our six and four-year-old girls (but obviously that could backfire with your teenager). I can't help but wonder if, as a culture, we've set the bar for gift giving too high. If you are making a direct correlation between how much you spend to how much you love someone... that will always let you down. This truth is also applicable to the quantity or frequency of gifts. If you measure love by how many gifts you give or how frequently you are purchasing something for someone, it will always fall short.

As previously mentioned, our oldest daughter, Story, loves to engage in reclaimed art. For her 7th birthday we secretly saved a giant box full of random parts, pieces and scraps, unveiling it that morning for a fun activity together. For the next two hours we taped and glued it all into an epic castle complete with a flying dragon! Instead of producing more packaging in the landfill, we just decided to have some fun with the packaging we already had! Now, while those castles and crafts have long been recycled, the memories we made will last a lifetime.

One of the pushbacks I've heard over the years is "What if my spiritual gift is giving?" or "Giving is my love language!" The truth is there are thousands of ways to give that don't involve mass amounts of consumption. (Or any at all!) We are only limited by our imaginations. And if you're anything like me, you've got a drawer or a tub under the bed, or a bin in the top of your closet stuffed full of somebody's love language!

We must be careful that our "giving" doesn't become our "excuse" to scratch our consumerist itch. If gift-giving really is your thing, then your first task should always be to ask or research what someone might actually want. If you find this difficult, it may prove to be a helpful litmus test to see if you're giving out of selflessness or selfishness, because both are possible. Sometimes we haven't done the inner work of deciphering between the two.

Obligation is another reason we sometimes feel trapped into gifting. How many wallets, flashlights, or pocket-knives have you given your dad over the years? I recently overheard a conversation between two people who were frustrated that they never knew what to get their fathers for their birthdays. "If he needs something he just goes out immediately and buys it!" - one sighed. For the other group out there who loathes shopping, maybe it's time to have a "come to Jesus" talk with your family and friends about the system of giving we trap ourselves in. How might we all have a big DTR around our gift giving, like adults? [5]

Like the old Nintendo that keeps on giving, the base level question here is, how might we re-frame our values around consumption? Once we've located what it is that we value we can work forward from there. Whether that's a conversation about presents, grocery shopping or looking for a new pair of jeans. If your values are local, organic, Earth-friendly, free of palm-oil, free-trade, plastic-free, reclaimed... then put those words at the top of your list. The truth is you do this already, we all do. We all operate out of some set of values, whether those are bent toward loving our world and our neighbors or simply loving ourselves.

What might it be like if we shifted our values in the world from how much money we are saving to how much life we are giving? How might the people of Christ operate out of Christ-like convictions in relation to our planet and our brothers and sisters impacted by our consumption?

What if our top determining value and criteria for consumption was love?

CHAPTER SEVEN

Seeing the Whole Way Down

They came to Bethsaida. Some people brought a blind man to him and begged him to touch him. He took the blind man by the hand and led him out of the village; and when he had put saliva on his eyes and laid his hands on him, he asked him, "Can you see anything?" And the man looked up and said, "I can see people, but they look like trees, walking."

Mark 8:22-24

I remember the morning and the moment clearly that still shocks and saddens me to my core. After so many years of working my way around a dirty job site with a trash bag slung over my shoulder, bending over to pick up cans, collect metal, and clean up a bit... you can pretty much assume how some people see you. Some folks will treat you like their brother, but others always see you with some patch of "beneathness." Truth is, for most of history the dirtiest positions in life were reserved for the "dirtiest people," the servants, the slaves, the prisoners. After thousands of years of course remnants of these ideologies still linger among our psyches. Unfortunately for some, it's much more than that though, its outright vulgarity.

As I went about my business on this warm day, I had noticed the crew of guys working there. Mostly they were white men likely not too many years older than me. I found myself trying to give them some space while also attempting to get my job done, but about that time one man came a little closer to me and said, "You know that's nigger-work, right?" - and walked away with a smile.

I was shocked.

Stopped in my tracks.

I could not believe what had just happened. It caught me so off guard I didn't know how to respond at all.

But most of all it made me angry. Angry that people are still seeing the world with those sorts of eyes. Angry that this ignorant, racists, and hateful lens still exists in the world.

Ironically, the one characteristic I remember from this person was that he had a tear tattooed under his eye...

In Mark 8 Jesus is healing a blind man in Bethsaida. To heal the man Jesus does one of his favorite sight-restoring moves and uses his own saliva. But something mysterious occurs in the process of healing the man and his sight is being restored... "I can see people, but they look like trees, walking."

Was this an "oops" moment for Jesus? Did he not use enough spit?

I like to imagine that for one brief moment before Jesus completed the healing, with the very essence of God incarnate in his eyes, this man began seeing something typically unseen... a halfway point, a remnant of humanities' genesis, a bit of the oneness of creation.

Our salvation, our healing, is an on-going journey. As we continue to catch a larger, more embodied, glimpse into the kingdom of heaven, can we be open to the continual clearing of our eyes to see not only our own needs but also the needs of our neighbors? Are we open to Jesus healing us further, to see how our desire for more might actually cause the bondage of others? Can we focus this gift of sight beyond ourselves, to the very roots of our consumption and waste?

The People Trapped Inside

Then the Lord said, "I have observed the misery of my people who are in Egypt; I have heard their cry on account of their taskmasters. Indeed, I know their sufferings
- **Exodus 3:7**

Whenever we read Old Testament stories about the people of God suffering under the thumb of Pharaoh and the Egyptians, we almost always think of ourselves as the Israelites. We always position ourselves in the story as the people of God. But what if we aren't the ones making the bricks in this analogy? What if we are the ones with the whips?

There are an estimated 40,300,000 enslaved persons in the world right now. About ¼ of these slaves, approximately 10 million, are children. Yes, that's right, little children. About 80% of slaves today work in the labor industry areas of agriculture, fishing, construction, mining, and manufacturing. The other 20% are trafficked for prostitution and sexual exploitation. Millions of people are enslaved right at this very moment. Would you do something about it if you could? Would you change the world if you had a say or vote in the matter? Would you do it today?[1]

You may be thinking, "but we don't have slaves any longer, right? How are these numbers so large? Where is this happening? And what does this have to do with me?"

Great questions.

Our garbage isn't the only thing hidden from our sight as a society. We find that the endings (trash) *and* beginnings (manufacturing) of our resources are kept from our observation as consumers. In fact, in the case of most of the goods we possess, we aren't present to experience its beginning or death. We're unfamiliar with its birth and its burial. As it turns out, it isn't just where our things "go to die" that's concealed, but we are frequently oblivious about their birth as well.

It does cause one to wonder…

Why are these origin stories so unknown?

Where does it all come from?

Who sewed this together?

Who was it that dug into the Earth and pulled out this mineral?

Who cut down the tree that made this chest? Who crafted it?

Who stuffed this toy doll?

Who screwed and glued and assembled all this together?

Where does it all come from?

Deep in the jungles of the Congo, hidden away from anything you and I will likely ever see, are the human faces that pay the hidden price so that we can purchase many of our consumer goods. Scarred, beaten, trapped and dying, villages of people just like you and me are living their lives in modern day slavery. People in all corners of the world live their dramatically shortened lives mining conflict minerals for our smartphones, cleaning fish for our dinners, smashing ore for our gold and diamonds, and making bricks in ovens resembling Dante's worst version of hell. Modern day slavery is happening right this very moment and we in the West are the slaveholder's biggest customer.

When I first began to learn about the slavery that was going on today in the world, I could hardly believe it. It sounded like something from antiquity, it sounded like a movie I'd seen or some novel I'd read. It didn't sound real.

But once you start asking questions you find answers.

Once you start knocking, doors open.
And you may not always like what you find.

It is a very difficult thing to accept, that so many of the goods we purchase from all over the world represent people with boots on their neck. The whole idea of slavery today is challenging for our western minds to compute. Haven't we left slavery behind by now? Aren't we evolved enough, smart enough, woke enough to not have slavery in the world? How is it that this is still happening? [2]

The truth is, we've evolved just enough in the world to know how to have slaves for just the right things, and a cunning group of the wealthy elite have grown "smart enough" to know how to hide it. In order for us all to live "so well" there are certain human structures out there making sure we get the opportunity to live as large as we desire.

We were arrogant to think we could all live like Pharaohs and that there wouldn't be a cost.

Back at home Walmart is rolling back prices. There's a BOGO deal at Captain D's. TV's have gone on sale for one weekend only. Meanwhile, our great pyramids of comfort grow taller and taller. We keep accumulating more, acquiring the next edition, upgrade, update, with better mileage and a longer-lasting battery. We keep purchasing clothes that wear holes in them after a few months. We shop and consume just because we're bored and it's something to do. The wheels just keep going around. And as long as we *need* our goods to be cheaper, someone somewhere will *have to* bear that cost, and you can bet it won't be the big corporations.

This Tuesday evening, somewhere in the world, one family is sitting down together, eating a healthy meal and watching a movie on their 46-inch smart TV before bed. They're tucked into their air-conditioned home full of every belonging you could possibly need in life, plus a garage full of things forgotten. At the same time, thousands of miles away, another family, possessing nothing, coughing from inhaling mine dust for the last 12 hours, gathers to receive their one meal for the day. A single bowl of lentils. After a brief moment of rest a boot begins hitting their legs. A father picks up his bag and begins the six-story climb back down the shaft, two children return to their scrubbing jobs, and a mother tries to disassociate as the slave-master forces her to surrender her body to his sexual appetites.

This perhaps all sounds stark and hyperbole, yet these narratives are real and occurring right now. Author and Professor of Contemporary Slavery, Kevin Bales, has written extensively on these issues in his work, *Blood and Earth: Modern Slavery, Ecocide and the Secret to Saving the World*. The problems here are deep and wide. It involves corrupt or an insufficient amount of law enforcement. It involves systems of modern-day peonage where slaves accumulate avalanches of debt just to meet their basic needs that can never be worked off. Even if miraculously one did, there's most certainly a gun pointed at their head.

In many situations, such as the forest clearing slavery happening in the Amazon, people are treated like single-use cups: used and then thrown away. This is even more possible in places of extreme poverty where people are desperate and vulnerable. In other places families in dire need of work are lured in by fast-talking promises of wealth or the chance of owning a plot of land, only to be stuck in these camps for life. Children grow up knowing these slave mines and quarries as their only reality. Families become trapped in hereditary debt bondage slavery that goes on for generations. It is truly the most heartbreaking reality in our world today, that there are so many souls shackled and tortured to produce our goods.

This is not to even mention the thousands of sweatshops that are somehow still allowed to persist in our world today serving the manufacturing and sewing demands for big-name companies.

If that new shirt only costs $6, somebody is not getting paid. Something unholy is happening somewhere.

In contrast, the money saved by companies and individuals coercing slave labor doesn't actually benefit the local economies in those regions. Slavery today is around a $32 billion industry annually. That amount is trivial in the grand scheme of our world economy. If we ended slavery today, the economy would be doing better than ever. Slave labor is a very low producing and inefficient way to manufacture in our time. When slaves are freed and given enough money to begin supporting themselves local economies begin drastically improving because more people are spending money. Ironically, everyone benefits from this, even those who were receiving the free labor. [3]

Perhaps unsuspectingly, modern slavery today goes hand in hand with the degradation and pollution of our world. Kevin Bales writes, "If slavery were an American state, it would have the population of California and the economic output of the District of Columbia, but it would be the world's third-largest producer of CO_2 emissions, behind China and the United States." [4] If we ended human slavery today it would be like taking a giant leap toward ending global warming. Slavery and unlawful environmental practices go hand in hand. By beginning to enforce and fund existing universal anti-slavery laws we would be protecting the environment from illegal deforestation, mining, kilns, and more. Helping our brothers and sisters escape slavery, in turn, begins to release the Earth from bondage from many of the harmful environmental practices that only exist through means of slaves! [5]

So, could you and I stand together to end it?

Our lives are woven together in a sacred nine billion thread tapestry. We are intertwined with the lives of so many others all over the world. To think that we simply go about our day working, shopping, and eating affecting only our own lives, is a myth! We live in a world economy and when you and I make choices about how we are going to live… it directly impacts hundreds of people.

The bad news here is also the good news.

No matter how long the chain is between that suffering family all those miles away and you, no matter how many corrupt systems and suppliers connect us, the buck stops with you. Quite literally, you, as the purchaser with the "buck" in your pocket. You and I as consumers wield a power and vote in these matters greater than anyone.

The desire controls the need.
We control the desire.

We control much of the outcomes just by what we eat, what we wear, and how we choose to shop. It's hard to really believe that our story could be so interconnected with the lives of people in situations like this. But our ignorance doesn't change the reality. Lives are lost at the expense of our gain.[6]

There is a deep connection between how we do industry, transportation, agriculture, electricity, and simply how we live at home and love our neighbor. We must understand that we live as part of an economic system that is driven by resources extracted from the ground beneath our feet... or rather, from underneath someone else's feet, often on the other side of the world. These extractions and manufacturing processes are intentionally hidden from us because, well, if you were selling goods that came off the backs of slaves and destroyed the Earth, I don't think you'd want to advertise that either. Most companies are professionals at keeping the faces behind these products from our sight. The true cost of our consumption hardly ever looks sexy enough to show.

This has led to long-standing segregation of our consumption practices from the lives of our brothers and sisters. This unholy ignorance must be shaken awake and given sight. Because everything we've ever decided to possess has come with a cost to the Earth and its people.

There is no good consumed that is separate from a human life and the life of the world.

There is no commodity without consequence. Be it negative or positive.

The meat on our plate. Tomatoes on our sandwich. Clothes on our back. Cars we drive. The wood in our walls. The electronics in our home. It all originates from some location in which people are involved and natural resources are harvested. Everything from the coal that we mine for our lights, to the coltan that is part of your phone is from the ground beneath our feet!

This may sound elementary, but this truth sits at the core of every single possession we have. The ways in which we choose to invest our money on a daily basis alter the course of people's lives and the life of our planet. Billions of consumer decisions every single day are shaping the course of history... In fact, if Earth's history could be squeezed into one single year, modern human life has existed for only the last 37 minutes and has already used up a third of Earth's natural resources in the last 0.2 seconds! [7]

Every choice you make matters. This is what holy living reminds us of.

But the goal isn't to remove our footprint from the Earth, that would be impossible. We must change our posture in the world. Returning to our creation story in Genesis, we see that it's not about taking ourselves out of the world, but our God-given initiative is to be participants in transforming it into something better, to protect and serve.

Our idea of "pro-life" needs to be broadened. To be *truly* pro-life is to show love right now in the ways you choose to live. Our consumption choices directly impact countless people today and unborn children of tomorrow. I think of my two little girls and all the children who are innocently waiting on the "adults" to begin caring for God's creation. Now is the time for God's people to act.

This information is challenging. It can feel overwhelming and anxiety-inducing. If you're anything like me the bubbles, we spent the first half of our lives in just keep getting burst. There seems to be no end to the kinds of injustices that revolve around our consumerism.

The easiest reaction is to shrug your shoulders and say, "It's all just too much to think about." "I can't save the world." "God's in control." "Jesus is coming back soon."

Theological scapegoating may be the church's greatest sin. If we aren't a little frightened by the thought of permanently altering our climate, we perhaps should be frightened of harming our neighbor and creation itself all, unrighteously, in the name of Jesus.

> *"One great reason why the rich in general have so little sympathy for the poor is because they so seldom visit them. Hence it is that [according to the common observation] one part of the world does not know what the other suffers. Many of them do not know, because they do not care to know: they keep out of the way of knowing it -and then plead their voluntary ignorance as an excuse for their hardness of heart."*
> **- John Wesley** [8]

It's a cycle as old as the Bible, the very arc of Scripture that reminds us of how we always forget and always marry the empire again. Israelites begin acting like Egyptians and are exiled into Babylon. The people of God are eventually set free only to repeat the story. The Roman Empire of Jesus' day was just the new upgraded model of this pattern of forgetfulness and exile. In our wealth and comfort, we tend to forget what it's like to be oppressed. Let's not be too surprised that we'd find ourselves here again in history.

Down Stream

You are cursed with a curse, for you are robbing me—the whole nation of you! Bring the full tithe into the storehouse, so that there may be food in my house, and thus put me to the test, says the Lord of hosts; see if I will not open the windows of heaven for you and pour down for you an overflowing blessing. I will rebuke the locust for you, so that it will not destroy the produce of your soil; and your vine in the field shall not be barren, says the Lord of hosts. Then all nations will count you happy, for you will be a land of delight, says the Lord of hosts.
- **Malachi 3:9-12**

The town of Morrisonville, Louisiana was founded in the late 1870s after the civil war. Freed slaves from plantations nearby went there to build new lives together. Quite literally in their newfound freedom they gathered and constructed new homes and new schools for their children who had no options for public education. It was supposed to be the beginning of a new era of opportunity.

After the war it *seemed* that the battle over slavery was finally finished, but in reality, the fight against racism had barely begun. Over the next 100 years as America's continued growth and industrialization unfolded, large companies were on the hunt for spots to put these new mass-producing factories. One by one these chemical plants and oil refineries were built along the predominantly black 85-mile stretch of Mississippi River between New Orleans and Baton Rouge. With over 150 of these facilities perched on the banks of this stretch of river it is now well known as Death Alley (or Cancer Alley). Down this alley grew alarming rates of death by cancer and other pollution-induced ailments that swept through these black communities year after year.

It was in 1959 that the Dow Chemical Company moved upstream from Morrisonville into Plaquemine, Louisiana. Dow began mass producing vinyl chloride, a colorless cancer-causing gas used to produce a variety of plastic products. As a result, it was only a matter of time before chemical poisoning took place in the water wells of Morrisonville. In short, this was the beginning of the end for this little town. Today all that is left of Morrisonville is the old cemetery. A memorial of those first pioneers of black freedom in America.

When a minority-group community populated primarily by people of color are burdened with a disproportionate number of garbage dumps, toxic waste facilities, and other origins of pollution, this is called environmental racism. All around the world these places exist where minority groups are carrying the brunt of the contamination, illness and disease that result from higher exposure to waste and pollution. If you've never lived in a place like this it's hard to believe that such injustices exist… but for those who have grown up in these fence-line communities, they know first-hand how toxins easily find their way into the air we breathe, the water we drink, and the ground we grow our food. [9] History has shown how the communities whose voices we never hear are the chosen landing zones for our waste. It is those who have little to no power to stop these contaminating systems or move elsewhere who fall prey to a life cut short.

For ages, people of color and those on the fringes of society have been receiving the environmental brunt of the waste of modern development. Morrisonville and the throng of those along the Mississippi River are unfortunately not isolated cases. Studies have shown that black Americans today are more exposed than white Americans to every single form of air pollution. [10] "Asthma Alley" is another such place in the South Bronx, New York. Here marginalized neighborhoods are surrounded by highways and diesel trucking companies that emit vast and constant amounts of exhaust onto their homes, businesses, churches and schools. The people who live here need asthma hospitalizations at five times the national average and at rates 21 times higher than other NYC neighborhoods.

In the Southwest corner of the United States indigenous communities have been suffering from the outcomes of environmental injustice through uranium mining for half a century. This highly radioactive material began to be mined and milled around and on indigenous land beginning during the Cold War. Some of the indigenous tribes even helped mine, even though they were underpaid and lacked the proper safety equipment. Meanwhile, these communities were not informed about the health hazards that scientists and government officials knew about at the time. What these indigenous people were left in the end with were not riches, but kidney damage, bone cancer, birth defects, and liver problems.[11]

Another vivid example of this is in Port Arthur, Texas. Here lies one of the largest oil refinery complexes in the world. It is also home to one the largest populations of disadvantaged and marginalized people living in fence-line communities. For about six decades now these massive refineries have spewed forth benzene, carbon monoxide, sulfur dioxide, and other pollutants at their leisure into the 95% African American area, often disregarding any clean air regulations. As you can imagine, the results are an array of health problems, including higher mortality rates and birth defects.

More familiar to some may be the majority black and low-socioeconomic town of Flint, Michigan. A couple years ago myself and a few others joined with some pastors in Flint and held a creation care summit; it was eye-opening to say the least! In some ways Flint has become the new ground-zero for readdressing environmental justice and racism for the American people. Today it seems that everyone knows a bit about the water crisis in Flint.

From the 1930's to the 1960's the black community in Flint was subject to red lining.[12] This Federally sanctioned act of racism left the majority of African Americans there segregated in areas of the city that were deemed distasteful or tainted... sometimes called "Colored Property." Decades later when the motor-industry boom was over most of the white people left, but the black people could not.[13]

So the stage was long set for environmental racism to culminate in 2014 with the water crisis. When the local government was taken over by a state appointed city manager due to financial insolvency, he decided to cut corners in the plan to save money by changing the incoming water supply from the Detroit system to the Flint River while a new pipeline was constructed and eliminate a necessary but expensive step from the water treatment process. Part of the motivation for this was because Flint had some of the highest water bills in the country due to poor infrastructure and price gouging by the city of Detroit, who was in a financial crisis themselves. It was long before 2014 though that the pollution began; the Flint river had been long subjected to waste run off from car manufacturing, chemical contamination, and industrial waste pollution. Eventually the incompetence, carelessness, and greed of the car manufacturing industries' appointed city manager, and a financially restricted local government paid full dividends against the innocent people of Flint. Now children who suffer lead-poisoning will pay the price for the rest of their lives. Where do you go when you can't afford to leave? How do you defend your home when your voice goes unheard? [14]

In developing countries where waste regulations barely exist there is an excess of toxic waste dumping. Globally, each year we produce up to 50 million tons of e-waste (electronic waste). That's about 150 times the weight of The Empire State Building! (*It's almost as if this stuff were designed to be discarded...*) This is an unholy amount of disposed electronics. (By the way, e-waste is anything from air-conditioners to washing machines to your laptop.) 80% of that e-waste globally is exported to Asia but astoundingly only 20% of the e-waste generated is recycled. The rest is either dumped, traded, or often it's recycled under inferior conditions in poor communities where mercury makes its way into rice fields and makes the water unfit to drink. Improperly disposed electronics also release vast quantities of greenhouse gases into the air. Our electronic waste is only one example of the great disparity of how the byproducts of our over consumption practices are impacting the lives of people of color and the voiceless all over the globe. [15 16 17 18 19 20 21 22]

As our climate is being altered from our over-consumption, it is the soaked streets of New Orleans to the vulnerable islands of the Philippines that are paying the price. Worldwide, it is the poorest communities who are affected most by this man-made climate disaster. These harmful effects are grossly unequal as the wealthy fail to control their carbon emissions while small vulnerable populations are left to be swept away by the results.[23] [24]

The problem of inequality has become a greater concern than ever before as we, in the global north, with less than 20% of the population are responsible for 70% of global emissions. Those most affected by environmental degradation are the people least responsible people for creating this brokenness.

Solving issues of racial inequality go hand in hand with solving issues of environmental justice!

We should not be surprised that defending the poorest communities on Earth, as God's people are called to do, helps restore balance to the whole thing.

Are we surprised that loving people as Jesus loved rights all wrongs, in all forms?

What if what God was upset about in Malachi 3 is that there was literally no food in God's storehouse? Verse 5 gives the context: "I will be swift to bear witness... against those who oppress the hired workers in their wages, the widow and the orphan, against those who thrust aside the alien, and do not fear me, says the Lord of hosts."[25] Robbing the Lord has always been about not taking care of those on the margins. And likewise food in the Lord's house has always been connected to the health of our "soil" and our "field" ... aka creation.

There hardly seems to be a person of faith who would not agree that our calling as a people of love exists to be the good news to the poor, the destitute, the voiceless, and the least of these. So how are we going to respond to these man-made gehennas, as a people marked by the kingdom of heaven?

Holy Consumers

Then the righteous will answer him, 'Lord, when was it that we saw you hungry and gave you food, or thirsty and gave you something to drink? And when was it that we saw you a stranger and welcomed you, or naked and gave you clothing? And when was it that we saw you sick or in prison and visited you?' And the king will answer them, 'Truly I tell you, just as you did it to one of the least of these who are members of my family, you did it to me.'
- **Matthew 25:37-40**

As we left the garden of Eden, the experience left in us the propensity to find our own way. We find ourselves with the tendency to trust in our own image to save us and in that we've drawn closer to a posture of wastefulness. A misuse of our lives, of our time, of our resources, of the very ground we live on. We consumed the fruit of the knowledge of good and evil, and it feels like we've been consuming everything we can ever since...

What if Jesus came to show us the path toward holy consumption? What does it look like to consume in good and appropriate ways?

There once was a time in history when we all knew where our goods came from. We had our local shops and suppliers; the world was a small place and we lived in small communities. Hundreds of years ago we were a people of trades and skills that met each local need. It was the real-life version of Settlers of Catan around here! Our baker was our friend, and our produce man was our brother.

Most of us probably aren't naive enough to think this model can be or should be a model for society today, but that shouldn't stop us from learning about who our new suppliers are. In fact, knowing the who, what and where of our products and produce is one of the ways we can know how to vote about the future and for the healing of our common home.

The ones who lead us into healing tomorrow are the ones who are willing to ask more questions today. On the outset this may sound challenging, on the other hand, could there be an easier way to change the world? On one hand it requires a good deal of product research and knowledge sharing with others and purchasing intentionality. Yet, it can be as simple as changing from one product to another. In the end, we all should be asking more questions. Holy living is curious living.

Holy people are awake people.

Awake to the birth, death, and resurrection of the things they use, purchase and consume.

How does this product affect those down the river from me? How does supporting this company impact those across the world? How does throwing this item away potentially harm my neighbor?

We must collectively embrace the responsibility of our relationship with all materiality in the world. We must turn our attention off solely economic-based purchasing decisions to ethical ones. The selling point should never be the simple dollar amount listed, the fact that something is on sale at T.J. Maxx, or how much money we'll save on those shoes. We must do the hard work of responsible living. And responsibility goes far beyond saving money.

Christians above all must embody good financial stewardship *by first* loving our brothers and sisters around the world by the kinds of purchases we are making and consuming we are participating in! Even if it costs us more. Let us be about loving our brothers and sisters in the world over our own economic success. Let us be about loving our neighbors as ourselves.

It's not by chance that God took on flesh in the world and ended up hanging on a cross. The downward path of love is in direct opposition to the world's value systems of prosperity and success. Love always leads to losing your life for the other. Love always leads to sacrifice, to becoming less so that the other might become more. We've put a lot of effort in trying to explain what the cross is *doing* for us while often missing what the cross is calling us all to *do*.

What if, learning to die is the path to *not* wasting your life?

Could it be that we are still too caught up in saving ourselves? No matter how much we have to throw away in the process, it seems to be worth the cost. How much do we spend on our own survival? On our own comfort? This is nothing new as society continues to look up instead of down. The temptation will always be to look up to who might be doing "better," who has more, and compare other situations with our own. Rather than to look down, into the eyes of those without.

The posture of looking up will always make you feel frugal.

But the harder path is looking down. Looking down river to see those who may be barely surviving, to those who we may be harming, to those who have less, this is what teaches us what the next loving step can be.

The hardest part will always be to unlearn, undo, and empty out.

The doorway into the kingdom of heaven is a dying, our baptisms remind us of this. So how is it we are still spending so much effort on the betterment of our living, especially while our brothers and sisters around the world have so little?

It is a stark moment in the gospels in Matthew 25 when Jesus says that those who inherit the kingdom are the ones found faithful with their food, drink, clothing and time.

We are informed that there is a direct connection with the squandering and waste of the resources within our grasp and inheriting the kingdom of heaven.

A few verses earlier, "wicked and lazy" are the adjectives used to describe the unfaithful servant who doesn't invest the master's capital. We like to take these words and apply them to people we think aren't "pulling their weight" in society. However, Jesus reserves this message for those who stockpile, hoard wealth, and put it all in the nest-egg rather than loving the least of these. Could it be that some of Jesus' strongest words of judgment have to do with our relationship with our resources?

Because as we know, where our treasure is, there our heart is also. In other words, it's not that we can buy our way into the kingdom of heaven by the way we choose to invest, but that the ways we choose to invest are the *real signs* of what is occurring in our hearts.

James writes in his epistle, "Anyone, then, who knows the right thing to do and fails to do it, commits sin." (James 4:17)

There is no other way around it. If we are willingly apathetic towards the human lives who are affected by the production of goods and resources that we regularly consume... isn't that what we would call meriting judgment? It is the harming of another. Living unintentionally in the ways we use our resources is the absolute opposite direction of the flow of the love of Christ. Could our "unintentionality" become the blood on our hands that our God is hearing cry out?

How might we be a people of clarity, direction, purpose, and holy intentional love?

What would it look like for us to become holy consumers?

We all must consume to live. Consumerism is not a dirty word, but a necessary part of life. So how might we breathe life into the world through our consumption? How might we love our neighbors in the ways we consume?

"There is no employment of our time, no action or conversation, that is purely indifferent. All is good or bad, because all our time, as everything we have, is not our own. All these are, as our Lord speaks... the property of another; of God our Creator."
- John Wesley [26]

Respond → Visit SlaveryFootprint.org and fill out the survey to see what practices of modern slavery you might be supporting.

Respond → When the creation and the disposal of what we consume is hidden from our sight, it's difficult to see how it's harming others. Here are some places to visit and take action:

- FreeTheSlaves.net - Here you will find videos, resources, and prompts to action.
- Go to Youtube.com and type in "Slavery: A Global Investigation" to watch a documentary on modern slavery.
- Visit DoneGood.co to find shop products that do good for people and the planet.
- Browse: KnowTheChain.org to see a scorecard of how companies are addressing forced labor in global supply chains.
- Visit FRDM.co to learn about mitigating supply chain risks.

Other wonderful resources for taking actions and finding pathways forward into ethical consumer choices:

EndSlaveryNow.org
TheGoodTrade.com
FairTradeCertified.org
BetterWorldShopper.org

Respond → Watch *The True Cost* - a film about the human and environmental cost of our clothes.[1]

Reflect → If this is the first time hearing about environmental racism and injustices it can feel like quite a load to haul...

What about this bothers you?

Do you find that you are more bothered by how these facts confront your value systems or that these kinds of injustices exist in the world?

What are your reflections on racial justice being tethered with environmental justice?

One of the hardest things to hear is that "my way of living has been harming others." It's normal to feel defensive, but once we take a breath, we must begin asking further questions:

How have I, maybe unknowingly, participated in any of these systems of injustice?

How can my faith community become a place of hope for racial and environmental reconciliation?

What actions might the people of God take in changing the narrative and bringing food into God's storehouse for the life of the world?

A Litany of Confession

Oh Creator God, hear our prayer as we confess our sins before you.

We confess how we often spend more time playing judge and jury than loving our neighbors.

Oh Lord, we repent.

We confess that we've consumed more than we needed while others have gone without.

Oh Lord, we repent.

We confess that we've been more concerned with the status of our comfort than the wounds of the world.

Oh Lord, we repent.

We confess that we've justified our excess, even in the face of our brothers and sisters who have nothing, because we had the privilege of a day's work.

Oh Lord, we repent.

We confess that our selfish ideologies around fairness have left graveyards of unreconciled creation buried away from sight.

Oh Lord, we repent.

We confess that we have worshiped the idols of consumerism.

Oh Lord, we repent.

Our God, thank you that you are able to make our paths straight. Guide us we pray in the way forward as we seek to lose our life in order to find it through loving you and loving our neighbor as ourselves.

Amen.

Leftovers

Then Jesus took the loaves, and when he had given thanks, he distributed them to those who were seated; so also the fish, as much as they wanted. When they were satisfied, he told his disciples, "Gather up the fragments left over, so that nothing may be lost." So they gathered them up, and from the fragments of the five barley loaves, left by those who had eaten, they filled twelve baskets.
- **John 6:11-13**

What comes to your mind when you think of leftovers? We typically think of food, right? There is a good chance you've got leftover dinner from Tuesday in your refrigerator right now. There's nothing quite like re-heated burritos and cold pizza!

I know some people who just don't do leftovers. They might have a refrigerator full of food from previously cooked meals but will never eat it. Because sometimes there is a stigma we've stuck on leftovers, isn't there? We say, "it's just not as good," "it's old," or "it just… smells weird."

I say some things are just better after they marinate for a while! My wife makes fun of me, but I don't like to microwave our leftovers. If you can eat it cold, you're already saving energy you didn't need to use. Also, call me a conspiracy theorist, but microwaves just ain't natural!

Leftovers are culturally unnatural for us now. In a time when we can DoorDash our dinner, get Blue Apron ingredient boxes at our door, find the nearest golden arches… for some of us our kitchens are just places where tumbleweeds blow around. "New" is not only made easy for us, but it can also be cheap. This goes for our dinner or the many gadgets that fill our homes.

We are almost all familiar with the story of Jesus feeding the 5,000. It is one of the few moments of Jesus' ministry that appears in all four Gospels. Jesus has been teaching the people for days and there arrives a point where people are hungry. Now imagine thousands of people had been standing around listening to Jesus talk for hours about love, grace, patience, and how blessed the poor are. Also imagine there are fishermen, mothers, children, and people from all sorts of trades. I'm guessing more than one or two people had brought a sack lunch on this spiritual quest out there with Jesus. Do we really think there were close to 10,000 people (counting women and children!) and only this one little boy had brought a snack?

Dare to imagine what thousands of people who had been listening to the life-giving words of God incarnate for days might do when in their hunger they see a small boy donate his meager meal to the cause? I would imagine it inspirational to say the least!

I would like to suggest that this moment here in John's Gospel is a miracle in which thousands of people began sharing their food. Bread and fish are taken and given as baskets are passed around the crowds. Would it be any surprise for our God to perform this miracle this way? Of course not, God is always working in the world through God's people. God's creation always seemed to be the vessel through which God works. Water is always what becomes the wine. So thousands of people get hungry and decide to put into practice this posture of love and the giving they've heard all about. The feeding of the 5,000 was a great moment of communal sharing and feasting!

Could there be a better image of the kingdom of God than the sharing of resources of the people of God?

Yet, I wonder if the most powerful moment here may not be when thousands of people are fed but maybe the small little moment afterward. Thousands of men, women, and children have just been miraculously fed and as the smoke clears there is a little clean up to do. It is here that something very important happens. Jesus tells his disciples to go gather up the leftovers so that nothing is lost. For Jesus, no fragment should be left behind. Remember, the kingdom of heaven is about zero-waste. For Jesus waste is out of the question and the leftovers are part of the ministry to come.

This story doesn't just end with everyone having their fill, but there is more food than they need. And anytime there is more in your hands than you need, that's God's call to ministry. This is the beauty that occurs as the people of God open their hands. That when we all open our hands for the needs of others, as it happens, there is more than enough for everyone. It is the miracle of love.

Essentially what's taken place here in John's gospel is a love offering where there's more love than need. In the end, is there any coincidence that twelve baskets of fragments were left? How perfect that each disciple would have his own basket of leftovers to share! I can only imagine as they journeyed on from there how they were able to continue feeding the masses. The more you and I are content living with simply enough, the more there will be left to feed the whole world. In a kingdom of God economy, there is no waste and even our leftovers go into the hands of our neighbors. If we see the world through the lens of scarcity rather than enough then our supplies will always be found wanting. But a kingdom economist would tell you, freely you have received, freely give.

CHAPTER EIGHT

The Fermata

Praise the Lord!
Praise the Lord from the heavens;
praise him in the heights!
Praise him, all his angels;
praise him, all his host!
Praise him, sun and moon;
praise him, all you shining stars!
Praise him, you highest heavens,
and you waters above the heavens!
Psalm 148:1-4

The Dance of Delight

Our planet is hurting, there is no doubt. The kind of issues we are grappling with here can create a heavy sense of urgency on our part to get to work. The expanse of healing that needs to happen in the world can give way to feelings of being over-whelmed. It's no secret how many people deal with depression and anxiety today. In the western world I can't help but believe some of this is due to the villages of concrete and steel we live in that isolate us from creation and the natural world, thus giving us feelings of isolation from our Creator. For the first time in history we actually have to be intentional about spending time in nature. We live in individually isolated temperature-controlled environments. In our homes and workplaces we can make it feel however we want when we want. It is light or dark at our command. The great fluorescent lights rise and set at our fingertips. We can further distance ourselves from nature and eventually find ourselves so acclimated for indoors that we struggle to be outdoors. This is why green spaces and parks are not only central for the life of the world but also for the health of our minds and souls. I believe that we must all curate that sacred time and space in our own individual lives to be in nature. But beyond that even, we must be people who *delight* in the natural world.

Returning to Genesis to retrieve a more holistic grasp on the creation narrative is vital for us to move forward with a proper perspective on our relationship with the Earth. But if we fail to retrieve the original delight that is part of the Image we are created in, we're still missing a crucial part. We've spent time understanding the meaning of the term *tov* and what God calls "good." But *tov* isn't just God's utilitarian term to use and pat himself on the back and say, "good job." God calls creation good because God is taking pleasure in creation. I can imagine God declaring "Yes this is good!" as another part of creation unfolds beautifully in God's presence and by God's creative initiative. God enjoys creation.

Being made in the image of our God reminds us that we are also made to enjoy creation. Delighting in the natural world around us is part of what makes us more wholly reflect our maker. There is something centering and sacred as we stand surrounded by nature, breathing, and ourselves declaring, this is good. Through God's people, God continues to call creation good. The joy is ongoing as we were created for this paradise.

Our sin occurs when we only see creation for how we can use it rather than as a source of joy. The natural world is yet another thing we objectify. Sin always objectifies. It is that first sin set on repeat, the consumption assumption. This is our downfall, that we too often believe our role is to have power over creation, rather than the sort of "power" that God exhibits toward us, a power embodied through love. The more we treat creation as an object rather than a subject, the more we will find ourselves disgruntled rather than delighted.

My friend David and I have had many discussions about the longevity of some of our clothing. I've had more than a few friends laugh at me (including my wife) at how old some of my clothes are! As long as there are no holes in inappropriate places it's still good, right? If I'm going to buy new clothes at this point in my life, there is inevitably a great deal of research that's involved. David and I have had a bit of fun sharing brands and finds with one another over time. One thing he said recently made me chuckle as he reminded me of the joy of creation. Speaking about the longevity of well-made clothing and his new pair of overalls that are supposed to *last a lifetime*, he said "you know it takes having them a few years before they break in, and you can really enjoy them!" He said while hugging his "overall-ed" body. We both laughed. David's joy over the simple pieces of creation should remind us all to take delight in every bit of it that surrounds us! There is no textile too small, there is no device too insignificant, there is no dish too little to delight in. We should stand in wonder and awe at creation and that we have the opportunity to be a part of it. We find joy not as we get to consume it, but as we acknowledge the intrinsic value of creation, and that we are in holy relationship with it.

The book of Job dates back to be the oldest Scripture we have, and its last few chapters are some of the most wonderful parts of this ancient text. After many arduous chapters of back and forth between the suffering Job and his friends, God finally says "Ahem, my turn!" Following this are pages of hearing God speak of the foundations of the Earth to the recesses of the deep, to the clouds, the sun, the snow and rain, the lions, the wild oxen, mountain goats, ostriches, horses and behemoths! On and on God presents a rhapsody of the wonders of creation! [1] It is no secret how wonderful and majestic God's works are. Scripture continually reminds us that our God is a God whose posture with creation is that of pleasure, not production. God is the great Maker who looks upon his work and smiles declaring, "this is good!"

Nothing reminds me more of this joyful relationship between us and creation than watching my two little girls running through our yard laughing and screaming. One of my favorite moments like this was one evening after a walk Emily and I sat on our front porch as it was getting dark and watched the girls play and laugh for a solid hour doing nothing else but throwing grass into the air and dancing. No toys, no lights, no music... just a yard and some bare feet.

When was the last time you delighted in creation?

When was the last time you danced in the grass?

When was the last time you ventured out into the forest and became swallowed by its goodness?

The Grateful Pause

The first time I ever saw the movie Avatar was in the theaters with my wife. Emily, who is the type to whisper little comments in my ear throughout an entire film, had said absolutely nothing through the whole movie. When the credits rolled, she finally looked at me and said, "that was awesome." You just never know what's going to grab you! There are many beautiful metaphors for us to grab in Avatar but one of my favorite scenes follows the native, Neytiri, who has to kill a wolf-like creature in defense of another. But instead of standing over the creature's body in victory, she kneels down and gives thanks for the creature's life.[2] For me, it is a reminder about our relationship with all that is created, even the seemingly vicious. What if, instead of trying to master and conquer the natural world, we co-exist in solidarity with it? This small sentiment represents a world of difference in how we can position ourselves as beings who must consume to live.

In my experience growing up we always gave thanks before each and every meal. If you grew up in a Christian home, there is a strong likelihood that you did the same. I love the simple moments of thanksgiving that we have before we consume anything because it is a call to stop and remember where it all comes from:

The hands of a loving Creator

who created fertile soil,

a farmer willing to work,

a truck-driver willing to deliver,

a baker willing to bake,

a shop owner willing to sell... all that we might have this bread.

We should be giving thanks. We are a people dependent on the gifts of creation and one another so that we might do something so simple as eat.

But it's not just food we should be giving thanks for. We should be offering prayers of gratitude for everything. As previously mentioned, everything you see, and will ever see has come up from the Earth. That is something to be thankful for. We must not just remember this moment of gratitude before we eat, but as we deposit that check, as we purchase those shoes, and especially as we eventually throw those shoes away.

In her show Tidying Up, organizational guru Marie Kondō helps homeowners simplify their homes and "purge" their mass amounts of belongings. But before just throwing items in the donation bin she always teaches people to pause long enough to express gratitude to your belongings for taking care of you.[3] I believe this is a holy practice as we remember where all matter originates.

What if before you ever took out the trash, you gave thanks for its life?

What if before you ever threw away that next thing you're about to get rid of, you stopped long enough to give thanks for this bit of creation that was yours?

Its life for your life.
Its energy for your energy.
It produced, and you consumed.

I'm convinced that if we could alter ourselves toward gratitude in the world around all that we purchase, burn, and toss-away, we would change the world quicker than you can imagine! Because when you are truly grateful for something, it's almost impossible not to care for it, not to give it value, not to be responsible with it, and not to love it.

It won't simply be technology that changes the world, or intergovernmental policies, or better recycling habits – no, it will be through the catalyst of radical gratitude that ultimately ripples healing change into our world.

And it starts with you.

How might we show gratitude for something, today?

Remember the Sabbath

Remember the sabbath day, and keep it holy. Six days you shall labor and do all your work. But the seventh day is a sabbath to the Lord your God; you shall not do any work—you, your son or your daughter, your male or female slave, your livestock, or the alien resident in your towns. For in six days the Lord made heaven and Earth, the sea, and all that is in them, but rested the seventh day; therefore the Lord blessed the sabbath day and consecrated it.
- **Exodus 20:8-11**

Stop. Take a breath. Close your eyes. Rest for a moment. Have you done that lately?

Sabbath is the gift built into our very DNA as the people of God that literally means *stop!* Instead of adhering to the societal norms that celebrate ceaseless work, citizens of the kingdom of God proclaim something very different. Our sabbath rest is a confession as well as a practice saying *we are not God,* and the world does not continue to turn by our doing and busyness. The universe, as it happens, is not dependent on our continual showing up!

Taking a sabbath becomes our act of faith in God and the world. Sabbath is a reminder of the rhythms of holy living, and how creation is wired this way from the beginning. God rests on the seventh day of creation and thus teaches us how to rest and that resting is also an important part of what it means to be a creator.

Sabbath reminds us that our identity is not found in what we consume, but in God. In faith, we take a day to stop. In doing so, we admit that our ceasing to...
work,
attain,
grow,
journey,
become,
produce,
accomplish,
achieve
...is not a waste.

Therefore, what actually occurs on the seventh day of creation is reflected by what good Jews say to one another every Friday night at sundown, "Shabbat Shalom!" Shabbat, meaning *Stop, cease, rest* and "Shalom," which is an expression meaning wholeness.

Shabbat Shalom!
"Wholeness to you! Thus, be at rest."

Blessing the leftover day, the empty space at the end, the time unfilled with stuff as "Shabbat Shalom" is pretty different than looking at this last day of creation and labeling it "a waste of time."

Stopping is not synonymous with wastefulness. But it is life-giving for us and the world as we confess and even relish the knowledge that Yahweh is God and we are not.

In the wilderness, the Israelites lived into this lesson every week and occasionally learned the hard way. In Exodus 16 we read the story of how God provided them with manna to eat and how they were to gather it. "The Israelites did so, some gathering more, some less. But when they measured it with an omer, those who gathered much had nothing over, and those who gathered little had no shortage; they gathered as much as each of them needed. And Moses said to them, 'Let no one leave any of it over until morning.' But they did not listen to Moses; some left part of it until morning, and it bred worms and became foul. And Moses was angry with them. Morning by morning they gathered it, as much as each needed; but when the sun grew hot, it melted." 4

The Israelites were provided for each day with "manna." They had just what they needed to live. It was all a gift. They simply had to do the work of collecting it. But if they left any manna unconsumed it would be full of maggots by the next morning, inedible. None of their food was meant to be wasted or hoarded. Every bit of it should go to use. Yet, as they went to collect their manna on the sixth day something extraordinary would happen! They were to gather enough for Friday *and* Saturday, the sabbath. This was their sabbath miracle, because doing this any other day would have resulted in rotten food for day two! The Israelites learned this lesson every seven days, their lives were in God's hands not their own.

Our journey with God has always been about us having just what we need for today. This has been a part of our story since the beginning as God's people. But in places where our resources don't rot the next day, in a time where refrigerators and preservatives tell us what we can eat, we feel more like the masters of our own destiny than the recipients of God's provision. Our separateness from the land and where our food grows further estranges us from the original tether and relationship with what the Earth provides for us daily.

When we choose to sabbath we are reminded of who we are.

Consumption is not who we are. It is something that we do.

Taking a day to rest has a way of reframing this for us. We can rest because our identity is found not in our needs, but in God's love and delight.

Oddly enough we often think that our drive to produce and consume helps us not be wasteful. We think if we cease then surely waste will ensue. On the contrary, the pause of sabbath is what prevents us from being wasteful. It is the necessary sleep pre-programmed into creation.

Waste is what happens when we never stop.
Waste is what occurs when we don't sleep.
Waste happens when we never pause to re-evaluate our

systems of production.

Waste is what occurs when we get to thinking that the world sits on our shoulders.

Waste is what happens when we try to be our own god, when we try to alter the natural order of created things, and when our "dominion" becomes an oppressive rule upon nature, rather than a loving stewardship.

So what happens to us and our world when we never get rest?

Kicked Out of the Garden

But in the seventh year there shall be a Sabbath of solemn rest for the land, a Sabbath to the LORD. You shall not sow your field or prune your vineyard.
- **Leviticus 25:4**

It is well known that we have to sleep to survive. It is well documented that around 10 days without sleep is all you're going to make it. To live is to sleep, to stop, to slow down, to breathe, and much of the natural world reflects this rhythm in some capacity. There will always be an inhale *and* an exhale to all of creation.

The more important query is what sort of state you're left in as you try to remain "awake." What does it mean to be an aware and functioning human being? At what cognitive level do we have to be, to be awake? Studies have shown that these are the actual lurking questions when someone tries to stay awake for long periods... what sort of awakeness will they have? Because there is almost always some cognitive impairment, some hallucinations, loss of motor skills, memory deficits, tremors, paranoia and even pain involved. Is it possible then, to be irresponsibly unrested?[5]

When we refuse to rest as a people...
to never press the pause button as a society...
to never put the brakes on the engine of progress...
What sort of progress could we really be making? What sort of work might we end up accomplishing in the world? Through the lack of these necessary rhythms, might our very industrial systems that we depend on be cognitively impaired?

When the people of Israel go into exile in Babylon, Jeremiah the prophet declares that they refused to allow the land to rest. In Leviticus 25 we learn that every seventh year the Israelites were to let the land rest, which as it happened, they did not do. *Can you believe it?* Much later we find that the consequences of unrest are exile...

In Jeremiah 25 the prophet declares there will be 70 years of captivity for the people of God. These 70 years were to account for every year the land hadn't been given its rest! Apparently, you can only abuse the Earth for so long before a larger cosmic order says, "no more!" The regenerative pattern of creation we observe in the very first page of the Bible, as it turns out, isn't open to suggestions. What perhaps is most powerful about the story is that Israel's land got its rest after all, even if it was through the very eviction of its tenants!

Eventually rest cycles around one way or another.

There is an undeniable link between our exile and the oppression of the land. It's no surprise that this command to care for the land and allowing it to rest is in our earliest commands in the Bible. Remember that we as humanity (*ha adam*) are taken from and tethered with the ground (*adamah*). We should all take pause today and contemplate this further.

Consider, might we also go into exile for the same crimes against the land that the early Israelites suffered all that time ago?

Is it possible that if we keep demanding from the Earth as if it's here solely for our plunder, that it might also find liberation by separating from us?

Is it possible that after non-stop, ceaseless and relentless extraction from the ground, that nature might send us a bill?

If we keep drilling for the forbidden fruit, will we eventually be like gods ourselves?
Or... might we find that there is no longer a place for us in Eden?

Respond & Reflect

Respond → This *Saturday, take a sabbath.*

For about the last 15 years my wife and I have taken off every Saturday for rest. Initially, you fight against it because you don't feel you have the time. Later, you understand that you don't have the time not to. When was the last time that you took time off? This Saturday, what if you just... didn't... do... much of anything? What if you rested from creating and consuming for a day as much as possible?

When the covid pandemic set in around the globe in 2020, people everywhere were documenting how clean the air was in places that usually were covered in smog!

How might your sabbath rest give respite to the natural world?

Could you take this one day to not drive around? To not shop? To not consume what you don't need to live?

Respond → Go dance in the grass!
Document your dance! #GarbageTheologyBook

Reflect → What are ways that you see sabbath and rest as tied to the healing of our world?

In what ways do you see an absence of rest as connected with wastefulness?

How might rest from creating and taking time to delight in creation make us into less-wasteful people?

CHAPTER NINE

Jesus Wants to Save Your Soil

As long as I am in the world, I am the light of the world." When
he had said this, he spat on the ground and made mud with the
saliva and spread the mud on the man's eyes, saying to him, "Go,
wash in the pool of Siloam" (which means Sent). Then he went
and washed and came back able to see.

John 5:5-7

In John 9 we read yet another story of Jesus healing a man
born blind, and again Jesus decides the best way forward is
through his very own saliva! But this time Jesus makes mud
and places it on the man's eyes.

Was the soil essential here? Is Jesus just trying to keep us on
our toes? I love this story because we are reminded of how
human Jesus is by the use of his very own bodily fluid, but
also how Earthy our healing sometimes needs to be. Could divine mud be God's chosen medium to give sight? God
breathes on the dust to create us and now is found spitting on
the dust to heal us.

As humanity, our healing is connected to the ground. By the
end of John 9 it is those who declare they have sight who are
discovered to be those truly blind! Maybe the blind receive

their sight because they are the only ones willing to be spit on or to have mud put on their faces and not care?

Healthy Humus, Healthy Humans

At some point, in order to see again, to find our healing, we've got to find ourselves in humble places. Places where the garbage has piled up, dirty places that need tending, ugly truths that need uncovering, and in small humble corners of the world. This is where a healthy garbage theology will take us.

Recently, out in the backyard with my daughter tending to our small garden bed, I found myself attempting to convey this simple connection. Naturally, when you have your hands all the way down in the dirt is when the best conversations come.

In the midst of weeding our garden bed and looking for worms, I explained that everything we eat comes from the ground. *insert six-year-old look of shock here* I went on to share the old adage "You are what you eat" – which is why it is so important for us to take good care of the ground. About this time we spotted a worm which usually involves some screaming. The worm proved to be a good segue for my lesson in microbiology, which naturally involved one of the great prophets of our day, Dr. Seuss. "Sweetie look! There are more living things in just a few tablespoons of healthy soil than there are people in the whole world," I explained. "Just like Dr. Seuss's Whoville, down in the good ground, far beyond what we can see is all this microbial life! And the healthier they are, the healthier we are! Because everything we eat comes from the soil, the better the soil is, the better food we have, and the better we are."

Naturally, in the simplicity of sharing with my daughter, I found myself connecting with this information in a primal way that I hadn't before. (The jury is still out as to whether we are teaching our kids, or our kids are teaching us!) Every one of our lives is dependent on good growing soil. So is this something we should be concerned about? Most of us who aren't farmers have never had the thought of our topsoil being a finite resource. But it is.

Plants and vegetation receive the majority of their nutrition to produce food for us out of that first foot or so of ground that they're planted in. That is where all the "good stuff" is. Even though many of us grew up learning how to use that old tiller, as it turns out, disturbing your topsoil this way actually decreases your yields. This was a big upset for me several years ago as someone who was raised behind a tiller! It's great to have loose soil, but when you till you are disturbing the healthy layers of your topsoil, and that healthy layer of soil eventually becomes depleted if we never take care of it. This very thing is happening on large scale farms all over the world.

When the soil is healthy, we are healthy.
When the Earth is wounded, we are wounded.

Learning about the current state of our world agriculture has been an authentic awakening in my life. The majority of agrarian scientists agree that at our current rate of industrial farming we have about 60 years of growing food left. Let that sink in. We are talking about around 60 more harvest years left on planet Earth. Farming and growing food as we know it is abruptly coming to an end due to topsoil erosion and desertification. Our patterns of tilling, monoculture, and pesticide use have left our fertile soil depleted and washing away.[1] [2]

To help explain this more, imagine your home garden if you have one. You're probably not just growing hundreds of rows of corn every year, but you have tomatoes, okra, beans, lettuce, among other wild things trying to make their way in. This is polyculture, where multiple things grow together at once. This is much closer to the way mother nature naturally works, right? The interchange is beyond what we can see. These plants, leaves, bugs, bees, and microscopic bio-life are all working together to give life to your garden through a community of God's natural design.

But say we decide we're just going to grow this single crop here (monoculture), over time this makes your soil and your plants more vulnerable to malnutrition and disease. So then what happens next? Pest control. We do our best to vaccinate our crops and spray them down with pesticides (which will now be in our food by the way). Now it seems that our crop will do better for a while until the disease makes a comeback and we need a stronger dose! Meanwhile, the soil is being depleted of all healthy microbiology and life. So, constant tilling, use of heavy farm vehicles on the land, and relentless pesticide use have left our soil vulnerable to the wind, rain, and evolving diseases (this is how we got the dust bowl by the way)! This is why no-till growing, cover crops, small farming, practices of cattle prairie restoration and permaculture are so important.[3] [4]

Globally we lose 75 billion metric tons of fertile soil from arable land every year.[5] On average farms are losing topsoil at a rate of 5.8 tons per acre per year. This number translates into crop yield loss and money loss. There is an estimated financial loss of 400 billion dollars worldwide each year because of topsoil erosion. [6]

It takes around 500 years to rebuild one inch of topsoil lost, and good crops require at least six inches on average.

This may sound like an oversimplification of a complicated issue, but the point being our soil is among our top resources being thrown away today. It is washing into streams, gullies, sewers, rivers, and flowing back into the oceans never to be seen again. How will we respond?

The Earth is running out of fertile ground.

Dare we confess that the sins committed against the ground today are far worse than that of our ancestors?

Currently, about 40 percent of the world's land has already been taken over by agriculture, and this percentage continues to grow as the search is on for more arable ground. With the planet now peaking at almost 8 billion people, we cannot afford to waste the very soil under our feet.[7]

Unfortunately, this issue is compounding as rainforests are being cut down for agricultural reasons because bigger-better agriculture is burning through rich soil like it's going out of style. Moving to deforestation for agricultural gain may be the definition of insanity. Yet, it is happening right now all over the world, and in places like Brazil it's happening on the backs of slaves. It's no surprise that the soil on these jungle floors is amazing. Places like the Amazon rainforests are modern day Edens, a seemingly endless network of plants working together to continually birth new life.

> *"The forest eats itself and lives forever."*
> - **Barbara Kingsolver**

We are removing these ecosystems from the surface of our planet at an alarming rate. These rainforests are our last great carbon sequesters; some call them the lungs of our planet. Even as we clear these forests and begin farming or cattle grazing there, the land will soon face the same fate as other conventional farms: overworked, chemical soaked, flowing away, degraded topsoil. Meanwhile, we are losing the carbon catching trees and simultaneously releasing the billions of tons of carbon that is currently stored inside the ground out into the atmosphere. Our planet's warming blanket of carbon dioxide is only thickening because of this method of agriculture.

Like so many other of the problems we are addressing, it is not readily apparent to the eye. If we look around, there seems to be dirt everywhere. But it's all about quality, not quantity. We can't necessarily see the microbiology that makes healthy soil, just like we can't visibly see the organic carbon being released into our atmosphere. We can only point to the side effects and the obvious outcomes. Erosion, pollution, ground compaction, waterlogging, acidification, loss of biodiversity, and salinity are all factors in the depletion of healthy topsoil. But solutions to this problem aren't a simple matter of now doing things on a larger scale, which is what got us here in the first place. It will without a doubt take many leaps of faith for us as societies and communities to take a second look at how we treat the land and grow our food.

It remains that our posture with the Earth must change. Whether you are a farmer reading this or an accountant, the bottom line is, you are a consumer. You eat food that grows from the ground. Unless we do some relearning about our relational framework with the Earth, there won't be much Earth to enjoy and there won't be many of us left to enjoy it. We must care for it so that it can care for us.

"The soil is the great connector of lives, the source and destination of all. It is the healer and restorer and resurrector, by which disease passes into health, age into youth, death into life. Without proper care for it we can have no community, because without proper care for it we can have no life."
- **Wendell Berry** [8]

Soil Solidarity

When you reap the harvest of your land, you shall not reap to the very edges of your field, or gather the gleanings of your harvest. You shall not strip your vineyard bare, or gather the fallen grapes of your vineyard; you shall leave them for the poor and the alien: I am the Lord your God.
- **Leviticus 19:9-10**

One of our current ventures here at home and in our lives that we are exploring is permaculture (permanent culture/agriculture). If you want to see a model of how the garden of Eden likely appeared, peer into permaculture! Permaculture, in many ways, is the opposite of monoculture. Monoculture focuses on growing this one single crop on a single plot of land, while permaculture may potentially grow thousands of different plants in a single space because it's about partnering with nature rather than putting it into submission. Permaculture is a testament to how well the Earth is designed to flourish! Through these ancient methods of agriculture, permaculture farming has been known to produce exponentially more food per acre than standard farming practices. Yet unlike other conventional farming methods, it isn't simply about following a set of gardening rules but is about returning to a sacred relationship with the land. There is a bit of a Pocahontas posture to it! Rather than boots on the ground digging for whatever "gold" we can extract, it resembles the familiar lyrics,

"You can own the Earth and still,

All you'll own is Earth until,

You can paint with all the colors of the wind."[9]

While this may be from a hit Disney movie, it does a great job of conveying a spirit of solidarity with the Earth. This spirit was present in so many peoples and tribes centuries ago, such as the Native Americans. Many of these ancient people groups understood more than anyone how we are dependent upon the Earth, and what it meant to listen to what it may be telling us.

Permaculture, before doing anything, begins by observing. This practice of stopping and looking returns us to this *tov-like* relationship with the Earth by first listening to the needs of the land just as you would a friend. Some permaculturists say that you should not begin any work until you've observed your land for at least a year! It is hard to imagine doing this in our fast-paced world. In our time the only stopping we do is a break for lunch! We are used to doing with the land whatever we want to do with it... building, planting, wielding anything anyway we choose. But what does my piece of land *want to do* naturally? What is already occurring and growing here?

How does the water flow? How might our plans join up with what already wants to happen here? What kind of soil is this? The discernment moves onward from there to eventually probe our own personal values and desires for our space.

Permaculture then isn't just some way of farming; it is a way of thinking. Permaculture is more than just attempting to be faithful and non-wasteful with our property, it is reflective of a way of existing in the world.

The core ethics here are Earth Care, People Care, and Fair Share, which are essentially what we've been addressing in this entire book. How we care for the Earth and how we care for one another are inseparably linked as we have discussed. The idea of Fair Share however gives us further clarity into how this interchange and relationship works. Under "Fair Share" are the ideas of *limits-aware* and *surplus-share.* These principles are about not taking more than you need, and if you have extra, then sharing it. Simple right? The most radical world-changing ideas are always elementary in a way. These truths are still the basic foundations we teach our children today. [10]

Fair Share has similarities to those familiar Biblical principles of allowing others to glean the edges of our fields. These are holiness principles ... precepts that are aware to how we are living responsibly as holy stewards of the land. How might we be a people more aware of our own limits and our own surplus in life? How many of us have more land or resources than we need? How many of us are still building bigger barns (Jesus had a pretty stark warning against this one)? A global example of this, as previously mentioned, is food production and waste.

The world currently produces exponentially more food than it consumes. Every year one-third of all food produced for human consumption globally is wasted. That's around 1.3 billion tons of food annually wasted through farming, manufacturing, distribution, retail, or residential loss. Wasted food is still the single greatest category of material that we throw into our landfills today. This is not to account for all the labor, water, and energy that we use to produce this food that gets wasted. The cost for this is equivalent to 2.6 trillion USD every year thrown into the garbage bin! Talk about inefficiency and bad economic sense! Again, with this much money, we could feed all the 815 million hungry people in the world several times over! [11] [12] This way of seeing begs the question, could there be something tremendously awry with our current systems?

The numbers suggest that we aren't having a bit of excess to figure out, but that we've drastically got something wrong. One recent example of this happened following the global spread of the pandemic, Covid-19. The virus inadvertently exposed so many broken systems for what they are. After the economy continued to struggle in the U.S., large-scale pig farming operations began shooting or gassing hundreds of "overstock" pigs. It was too expensive to keep feeding them or have them butchered. Also after several months the pigs become too large to even process. I'll never forget seeing the image of hundreds of pig bodies piled up high. But this wasn't an isolated issue during the outbreak. Millions of chickens were gassed, eggs were smashed, thousands of gallons of milk poured out, and vast amounts of vegetables were tossed. Meanwhile, people are needing food more than ever and we're scrambling to feed families who've lost their jobs. At one point we thought that a bigger industry was better. These tragedies are reflections of the problems at large. Great miscalculations have been made in the way we feed ourselves and consume in the world. [13] [14]

Could some of these foundational questions of permaculture be important for us today? When you start trying to feed billions of people by asking the wrong set of questions, you'll find that you continue down the wrong path from that point on. It begins to feel as if we are forcing a global food system to work, that just doesn't. The further we try to force-feed the ground, force-feed our cattle, and force-feed ourselves, we will find that we aren't "feeding" anyone.

My goat-whispering urban-farmer friend, Jason, talks about how small farming is in many ways the hope of the world. I believe he is spot on. Currently, Brazil is one of the only places in the world where the number of small family farms is growing. In the last 20 years, these have grown from hundreds of thousands to over a whopping 4 million family farms. These little farms produce 70% of Brazil's food on just

30% of the active agricultural land! On top of that, because these farms don't have big outstanding subsidies to large farm corporations, they make more money and are more efficient. Small farming also lends to more biodiversity and regenerative agriculture as they are rarely monoculture oriented and usually involve some form of livestock. Also, small farms are more able to conserve water and other resources as they're more agile than big agricultural businesses. Meanwhile, we are witnessing the ending of even more family farms here in America because of our broken food systems. Small local farms were our past, and agricultural experts say, must have a big role in our future, for the life of the world. [15] [16]

What might it look like, rather than bending the Earth to our will through our powers of technology and conventional industrial farming, to instead do some listening? What might it look like for us as a society to start with some essential values and work from there? Could feeding the world be more than a simple math equation? Could it involve returning to a primal relationship with the Earth? Could the nutritional well-being of all humanity be tethered to the nutritional well-being of the Earth? Is it possible for 8 billion people to have a regenerative relationship with our planet? I believe it is not only possible but crucial for the lives of future generations. We must move beyond simply a sustainable relationship with creation, into a regenerative and restorative one. We are, after all, a resurrection people!

Dumpsters

Then he told them a parable: "The land of a rich man produced abundantly. And he thought to himself, 'What should I
do, for I have no place to store my crops?' Then he said, 'I will
do this: I will pull down my barns and build larger ones, and
there I will store all my grain and my goods. And I will say to
my soul, Soul, you have ample goods laid up for many years;
relax, eat, drink, be merry.' But God said to him, 'You fool!
This very night your life is being demanded of you. And the
things you have prepared, whose will they be?' So it is with
those who store up treasures for themselves but are not rich
toward God."
- **Luke 12:16-21**

Dumpsters are some of my favorite spots. If you happen to
live around Nashville, Tennessee in the last several years
you've seen more than a few of these big metal tubs sitting
around. It seems everyone is tearing down their old barns to
build bigger ones! A large part of my work over the years has
been cleaning up active construction sites. Often for really big
jobs there's a dumpster on site ready to be filled. So, cleaning
up is a matter of figuring out what needs tossed and what can
I salvage. In a report by Transparency Market Research, construction and demolition waste are currently doubling to a
high of 2.2 billion tons of debris per year! In my city, construction and demolition waste make up 23% of all the waste
we send to the landfill! This is a mammoth amount of raw
material just thrown away. These dumpsters are filled to the

brim with wood, metal, drywall, plaster, concrete, shingles, and everything else under the sun! I see these giant boxes as modern treasure chests though. You can excavate enough material to do about any small (and sometimes large!) household project from fishing in one of these giant bins... although you may have to brush aside a dozen cardboard boxes that are tossed rather than recycled. (Watch for nails and don't fall in!)

At our home, we've completed plenty of projects with re-claimed material, including two decks and our tiny house! There is no end to what you'll find if you're willing to do a lit-tle scavenging. I've seen brand new doors, windows, studs, trim, light fixtures, tons of bricks, whole sheets of drywall, new insulation, cabinets, and much more still in the wrapper simply tossed away. The fact is most of these large construc-tion operations are just moving and grooving. Those who manage these sites hardly have time to return wrong orders, take items to donate, or find creative re-use for such a quan-tity of material. It's either being rescued by people willing to engage in some creative use or it's headed to the landfill.

Perhaps the only places where dumpsters might be more ex-citing are the ones parked behind grocery stores! Today there are entire communities of "freegans" who rarely go inside the store because food scavenging is such a big part of their life. Many go about their weeks recovering food from dumpsters that are expired but still healthy and good for eating. Grocery chains, restaurants and bakers toss bags and bags of "expired" or bruised goods that should instead find their way to hungry people. I have several friends here in town that frequent food bins and dumpsters and collect truckloads of a harvest each week! Obviously, one should use common sense about consuming rotten, thawed, moldy or spoiled food.

My friend Jason constantly has a truck bed full of "discarded" food. In fact, I'm not sure that he ever actually grocery shops! So much of the food that is discarded is still good to enjoy. An astounding 10% (43 billion pounds) of American grocery store food never even makes it off the shelf, while up to half of that is said to still be edible according to recent studies. Meanwhile, over 23 million Americans lack access to fresh produce. [17]

How might we re-envision what gleaning looks like in the world?

How might we waste less food and feed more families who are going to bed hungry tonight?

And how might we speak out against the irresponsibility of food waste?

Could it be that,

Holy living eats blemished vegetables and buys food with upcoming expiration dates?

Maybe holy living isn't afraid to scavenge through the dumpsters of our time to work toward food justice?

It's never been about having enough resources in the world. God's magnificent creation, though greatly harmed by our over-consumption, deforestation, and modern farming methods, is incredibly prolific. Living with "enough" doesn't mean that we are all barely getting by and living miserable lives! Planet Earth is more than capable of sustaining everyone here and more! It just needs to be cared for… something I think we can all agree on! The reason we are harming our planet while also not collectively living well is because we're trying to drive on the highway in second gear. We're going 20 mph and the engine is burning up. We are leveraging the soil for profit rather than for the life of the world. And we are discarding the produce of the soil before they even make it to the shelf because of how they look or throwing goods away because some business has given it a false "shelf-life."

Ultimately these postures in the world are incredibly inefficient. This is why learning practices like permaculture are so important for us all. To feed the world in the days to come we will have to break out of these past paradigms of "every man for himself" and "it's mine to do with as I please." We must learn to see the ground underneath our feet as God's, under the care of God's people, for the life of all living creatures and all future generations. [18] [19] [20] [21] [22]

Respond & Reflect

Respond → *Find a dumpster and look around in it for something usable!*

Could it be that one of the first things we have to overcome is a phobia of trash? Put on some gloves and see what you can find!

Respond → *Sign up for a local CSA from a farm in your area. Plan a trip to see the farm and meet the farmer.*

One of the greatest things we can do other than learning how to serve and keep our own land is supporting local farmers. Find a CSA (Community Supported Agriculture) and start getting your vegetables there. Let the farmers know how much you appreciate them!

Respond → *Visit www.misfitsmarket.com and sign up to receive odd-looking but tasty produce!*

Respond → *Go two entire weeks without consuming beef.*

Another great way to respond is by eating less meat. The less meat we consume, especially beef, the less land we need for livestock. Simply put, pastures for livestock currently occupy a whopping 26 percent of the world's (ice-free) land for grazing, and along with that one-third of global arable land is used to grow their feed!

Stop and think about this. Almost 80 percent of the total agricultural land in the world is dedicated to giving us meat. [1]

My family is not vegetarian; we do eat a little meat once a week or so. Although the meat that we consume comes from Trevecca Urban Farm down the street from us, or a local meat farm, or Gabby's - a local grass-fed burger place. Eating the right kinds of meat, from livestock that has been properly grazed and rotated is one of the top ways we can actually build topsoil and even sequester carbon back into the ground! While few large-scale operations do agriculture this way, it is possible!

When we first really scaled back with our meat eating as newlyweds it was truly a struggle. Because as a young American man, hamburgers and steaks were as naturally a part of my diet as sweet tea! Honestly though, after just a little while of not eating beef, I found myself only craving the fries! Not to mention they are some ridiculously tasty veggie burgers out there today that are good for you and the planet.

How did it go? Did you find other sources of protein (there are lots)? If you share your story digitally, use #GarbageTheologyBook to see how others made it!

Respond → *Watch a documentary!*

Kiss the Ground (kisstheground.com) and Just Eat It (food-wastemovie.com) are great films that deal with the issues in this chapter.

Reflect → We must begin to consider that our bond with the Earth is more than just people living on top of a planet. Our

God is much more creative than that! We've always been interwoven with the Earth, with one another, and made into the image of God. As you can see these issues of soil are widely social yet also very personal.

As the people of God, how might we lead the way in taking care of our land?
How is stewarding our agriculture connected to taking care of our brothers and sisters, in your own words?

How have you experienced your health being connected with the health of the soil?

How might we support better agriculture? What ideas do you have?
How might we ourselves interact with the ground in a holier way?

How do you see God's concerns for the land and people way back in Leviticus as still something God is desiring for God's people today?

Returning to the Ground

I'm not sure that there is a better or more natural-Earthy image of resurrection than compost. Composting is what happens when we take our food scraps, leaves, grass clippings and other organic matter and help it along the path to do what nature naturally does, decomposition. But when this composting process is done well, with a proper mixture of green and brown, carbon and nitrogen rich material, and the right amount of water and oxygen... you get a shovel full of heaven on Earth. We are often separated from our food sources in the world, but you can be sure that life springs from a good compost pile! This natural recipe created from decay supplies the necessary building blocks for the proliferation of new life and growth. If you want to start growing food in your yard, you should begin by decaying food in your yard. Again, this is the thumbprint of the Divine story imprinted on creation that says, Life, Death, and New Life!

What's interesting is what happens to our food when it doesn't get the chance to decompose naturally. When your food isn't giving life through the process of composting, it takes a sinister turn. In the United States alone 40 percent of our food goes uneaten... that's around 400 pounds per person annually![6] But what is unseen is what occurs when all this food gets trapped in oxygen and dirt-deprived landfills. When our leftovers get tossed into landfills it creates the toxic greenhouse gas called methane (which is exponentially more potent than carbon dioxide). Modern landfills are designed to attempt to capture and use this gas locally. But inevitably the food that has slipped from our crates and plates into these dark holes will find ways to leach these deadly fumes into our atmosphere. Not only that but the more food that is thrown away represents fossil fuels needlessly burned. Our systems of food production use vast amounts of oil. Oil is used on the farm, in making pesticides, in packaging and processing, and the transportation. Such a great portion of our food waste today is ultimately something we never see. These are the hidden sins of our overconsumption and waste.

Regardless of whether you care about this or not, what we should be focused on is how great it is to compost. Composting is a wonder among creation. That the pure natural occurring plants and vegetation on the planet can decompose in a way that provides amazing nutrient rich soil that we can grow with! In other countries such as Germany they've integrated this process so well within their municipal systems. But here in the states, we are still tossing volumes of compostable foods into our landfills when we could be putting these scraps to work for us.

Some U.S. cities and communities are getting really good at re-using human waste and food waste as compost. Done properly this sort of creative recycling of the basic waste that we are all producing daily can turn around and help feed many people in the form of good soil. For example, the city of Lynden, Washington converts biosolids into about 100 dry tons of compost a year and offers it free to residents![7] This one change has diverted hundreds of truckloads of human waste from landfills and breathes life into the soil of the community. In other places, small curbside compost companies are popping up that will come by and pick up your compost for you on a regular schedule. Later on, you can acquire some of the good soil for your use at home.

Our food isn't the only biological element that isn't getting the opportunity to return to the soil though.

At the end of 2020, after a long decade of planning, the very first full-service human-composting funeral home opened in the United States.[8] At Recompose, this new take on a funeral home in Washington, in just a handful of weeks, the body of your deceased loved ones becomes soil once again. While it's a weird thing to consider, might the very composting of our bodies be the "new" way forward?

Typically, here in the States when you die your body is placed inside an extra-plush shiny casket. Odds are this fancy new chariot is nicer than anything you actually drove when you were alive, except without the Bluetooth capabilities! But this Rolls Royce of death never even touches the dirt. The casket is lowered into a larger vault typically made of reinforced concrete. Once your casket is closed and your vault is sealed and there is six feet of dirt on top of you, dead or alive you ain't getting out!

Let us pause here for a moment. If this isn't your chosen path odds are your body will be either placed in an above ground mausoleum that is equally fortified, or you're cremated. (For those interested in such things, one cremation is the equivalent to a 500-mile road trip's worth of emissions.) I think if we are honest with ourselves... none of these options sound natural. That's mainly because, well, none of these options are natural. When I think about being buried in one of those cushy boxes and lowered into a vault, I don't care what you say... it's disturbing!

As a child I went to an exorbitant number of funerals. It wasn't until I was an adult that I realized how abnormal this was among my friends. As a family we just knew a lot of people and a lot of people we knew died. So, my best guess is that's why we were at a lot of funerals. Years into our marriage I remember confessing to my wife that I couldn't smell any bouquet of flowers without having vivid images of funeral homes. Even as an innocent kid, and perhaps only because it was from the perspective of a child, everything from the casket to the dark maroon curtains and low lighting, to the suits we all wore, to the way this person looked so pale and lifeless laying there... it was all so unnatural. Who in life would want to be in a setting like this? Why do we gather like this in death?

Imagine with me a beautiful forest. Deer and squirrels wonder about down paths near streams. The wind gently blows as family and friends gather. The deceased relative has been placed in a wicker casket that is carried down a wide trail deeper into the forest and buried there in the beauty of creation. Flowers and trees grow around the site and birds are singing a dirge up above. In only about six months or less the body will have returned to the Earth from which it was created. Today we refer to this as natural or green burial, but 100's of years ago this was, of course, just a regular burial.

This sounds beautiful, doesn't it? One of my favorite examples of this "new" system is at Larkspur Conservation in Tennessee. This natural burial site is located on a beautiful 172-acre biodiverse forest. This land is preserved and offered in memory of the family's father who owned and farmed the land. This beautiful offering now gives new life to seasons of death. [9]

Beyond caskets and land use, it must be stated that even our deaths can be "wasted." Our bodies are meant to be returned to the Earth. This frail skin and these organs are all part of the Earth from where they came. Our bodies contain iron, zinc, sulfur, calcium, and phosphorus that can enrich the soil. It's wondrous to think that our bodies might return to the ground. The *adamah* from which God breathed life into us, we finally return to in death. It is the exhale of God's life-giving inhale. Our bodies are meant to be a gift back to the Earth as we ourselves once again become life-giving compost. Yet, we live in an age that robs the Earth of our bodies after we are gone. Our concrete tombs prevent the necessary cycle of decomposition that we and the Earth needs. There are more people alive than ever before in history. Our cemeteries and our cremations are already altering the chemistry of the Earth and as billions more die over the coming decades this will be an issue we must address. So ask yourself, why waste your body? [10] The life inside us should be recycling in the soil we have so eagerly extracted from our entire lives. We've surely taken our share from the Earth in life; it is a travesty for us to keep taking from it in our death. How might the people of God embody hope for the world even through our death and decay?

Respond → For one week collect all your food scraps in a bucket and document the size or quantity. Imagine all of that going back into feeding the Earth rather than harming it.

#GarbageTheologyBook

→ Look into local companies and government run programs for composting in your area.

→ Start your own compost! There are plenty of online aids to learn about how to compost. You can visit epa.gov/recycle/composting-home to find out more.

→ Visit LarkspurConservation.org to see how natural burials work.

CHAPTER TEN

Hauling Your Load

Like good stewards of the manifold grace of God, serve one another with whatever gift each of you has received.

1 Peter 4:10

Growing up I watched the show Captain Planet and the Planeteers (clearly it had its effect on me)! The intro song is still stuck in my head:

"Let our powers combine. Earth."

"Fire."

"Wind."

"Water."

"Heart."

"Go, Planet!"

"By your powers combined, I am Captain Planet."

insert Captain Planet jingle that will never go away.

Five teenagers from around the world, possessing magical rings that gave each the power of a particular part of creation, fought against the evils of environmental maltreatment. When they put their rings together, superhero Captain Planet appeared to "finish off" the polluting villain of each episode!

I always appreciate how even a simple children's cartoon can tap into a universal truth. Not unlike these teenagers, we each have our own corner of the world, and each have different "elements" under our service. We all hold our own positions of power and influence that makes us part of the global team that must keep and care for creation. Only when we come together from our different places of passion, position, and power will we be able to once again be God's means of blessing and healing against all forms of planetary injustice.

You know, one thing that always struck me as odd in this show was, "Why is 'heart' an element?" Earth, fire, wind, water... all that made sense. But heart?

Could it be, that we, humanity, are the fifth element and it is our heart alive and in unison with the rest of creation, as God created it to be, that we will find our healing...

Sherry

The first day I met her it was scary. She was intense, serious, firm, and I didn't know whether to stand my ground or cower. Sherry works at our local recycling center just a couple of miles down from where I live. Because recycling was becoming a big part of what I was doing with my life... we were destined to be either enemies or friends.

Once she and I came to understand we were playing for the same team, and we were equally passionate about what we were doing, a true bond was formed. I've come through Sherry's gate many times through the years, and we've had countless little chats about the ins and outs of making the world better. But what I love about Sherry is that still to this day she isn't afraid to get in my face or give me a hard time if it seems I'm fudging the lines or not properly recycling! I've realized often that she will "put you back in your place" no matter how "friendly" it all seems!

I will always remember the day I accidentally let a rat loose in the recycling facility. Unbeknownst to me, it had been re-siding in a trash can that had been loaded onto the back of the truck and freeloaded a ride to rat heaven. As I was un-loading, the giant creature leaped from the trash can giving me a heart attack. Of course, Sherry, who sees all, observes the large beast running at top speed across the facility and comes out marching straight towards me... She yells at the top of her lungs, "Don't you be bringing RATS in here!" Some poor bystander, who was simply waiting to pay and unload his trash, gave me the look of pity as I endured the wrath of apparently committing an offense reminiscent of recycling treason. It probably didn't make matters any better that al-most the only thing I could do was laugh at the situation. In my mind, this wasn't as bad as the snake I found in the back of my truck and let loose at the center on the east side of town!

Sherry was hard on me in those early days because she was doing her job well. You see Sherry sits in her trailer behind a sliding window every day at the convenience center as the last line of defense. She stands between life and landfill, keeping watch as best she can to prevent a world of waste. She realizes the importance of her role and cares deeply about how we are treating the Earth. Yet unfortunately, she is almost the only person I've met over the years, that works in her position, that truly cares about what comes through their gates and isn't just there to pay the bills.

We've all got something to learn from Sherry. Her job description didn't require such fervor and passion, but she brings that with her because she cares.

What would it look like for us all to bring such care into each and every one of our vocations? What if each of us did our work each day seeing that we ourselves sit at a very particular doorway that no one else does? We could change the world.

No one else is you. No one else has your life, works at your desk, lives in your home. It is your role alone to implement serving and keeping God's creation where you are. You are the keeper of your part of the garden, no one else.

I can think of so many times when my wife Emily has done just this. We've hosted countless community events that were meticulously planned, from the biodegradable silver-ware to the paper cups, she thinks through everything! We've gone out of our way so frequently to make something zero-waste and be faithful with our little part of the whole. Because ultimately, every one of us is on the front lines of waste and consumerism. You are the doorkeeper of your domain, just like Sherry is the doorkeeper of the recycling center.

It will likely be difficult at first to start taking ownership in ways you may have never imagined before. In the beginning it may be a battle between Styrofoam cups in the breakroom and the budget committee in the boardroom. But at the end of the day, as pastors, recycling center employees, teachers, CEO's and everywhere in between, our vocations are the front lines of "good news" for the Earth or the catalyst of its destruction.

The Earth needs you to become passionate about this wherever you are!
What would it mean for you to stand at the door today, serving and keeping with fervor in your workplace?
In your home?
With what is in your hands?

By no means does this book have all the solutions to our world-wide waste crises, but I do know that each of us holds part of the answer. Each of us, in our own ways, must step into the matter of matter, and the artform therein. This is how we must see this work... not through a utilitarian eye, but a creative and zero-waste one!

May this care for creation be a curious work for you, exciting and full of passion! May the work call you to engage your corner of the world in ways that you've never thought of before! May something holy stir within you as you...
conceive,
invent,
forge,
order,
build,
and engage in the art of this waste-eliminating work in our world!

Hell Shall Not Prevail

And I say also unto thee, That thou art Peter, and upon this rock I will build my church; and the gates of hell shall not prevail against it.
- Matthew 16:18 [1]

I have some real fond memories connected to a particular church building from my childhood and a grassy lot that used to exist across the street. A few large smooth rocks rose to the surface in certain spots almost as if God intended them to be bases for kickball. We had more than a few Sunday night good times as kids there on that small plot of land the church owned.

But looking back as an adult I realize how isolated we were from that community. Hardly a soul from that poor community ever set foot in our unfamiliar building, and that grassy lot brought joy to no-one six days out of the week. In fact, eventually we gated off our parking lot from the neighborhood, reserving it entirely for church goers. (You know, liability issues.) It felt like such a waste.

Our lives and work are not the only areas where we have a responsibility as the last line in defense against waste; our local churches are the other place where we have an opportunity to care and protect God's creation and resources from waste.

During different seasons of my life, I've worn the official badge of church custodian. Being alone in old dark church buildings for long hours always hinges somewhere between holy and creepy! One of these seasons was during my collegiate years at a large local church facility. This was a full-time job that I took over the summer to make some money and keep the tacos coming! Because how else do you survive college? Throughout summer, I clocked in every day, grabbed my spray cleaners, vacuum and rags and went to cleaning. Yet as the weeks went by, I grew more and more frustrated with the job. It wasn't because the work was too hard or dirty, on the contrary, it was hardly dirty at all! I became increasingly discontented because it just didn't need cleaning! The building was used primarily on Sundays and then a small bit during the week. But even then, there was hardly much to scrub or wash. Inevitably, I ended up wiping down clean surfaces and vacuuming the same spotless floors again and again.

Eventually I sat down in my friend's office who worked at the church and exhaled my grievances. Not only was it boring, but I also felt guilty for taking their money. Mind you, I was about one of five custodians who worked full-time (the place is huge). I realized I was simply making the case that they didn't need me. Looking back, this conversation was not financially wise to say the least! My friend laughed at me as I shared my cleaning woes with him. After all, it was kind of comical!

When I mentioned my plans to have a chat with my "church boss" about it, he warned me not to. My friend said I would just cause frustration, and I would likely then be told to go around and start cleaning all the baseboards in the church... and of course, that's exactly what happened. That whole season of life meandered on, and the job went on as it had while I diverted some attention to changing out lightbulbs to mix things up a bit.

This story here, I'm sure, isn't an isolated one. It's a reflection upon the way we often use our resources in the church, the things we are focused on, and the spotless temples we're still upkeeping.

Could it be that we are so busy cleaning the inside of our sanctuary because we still haven't allowed our salvation narrative to be more than "spiritual"? Are we still struggling to connect that our God is a God also outside the holy of holies? If we've interpreted holy living as an attempt to be as perfect as possible rather than the messy work of daily walking with God, we've missed it.

It's no mystery that the kind of gospel message the local church often communicates is the same as the rest of the world, which is: *our resources are for us.*

But what if this was different?

What if the money used to clean this building was repurposed to do some street clean-up? What if the resources placed into keeping up these ever relic-like facilities, were mobilized to impact our communities for the kingdom of God instead? What would it look like to clean the baseboards of our community? What would it look like to take that money and pay for neighborhood custodial services? Or use that money to sponsor children across the world?

As the people of God, what if we became holy doorkeepers against waste? Using our little corner of the world and the resources in our hands to work creatively alongside God to utilize our parking lots and cleaning staff to proclaim God's love? What if instead of shutting off our sacred spaces we became protectors against these spaces being wasted 6 days of the week?

In the famous passage above, Jesus journeys with his disciples to Caesarea Philippi where there existed an infamous worship site to the Greek god Pan. If you go there today you can still see the site of this deep cave where rituals were performed to entice this false god. It would have been a familiar scene over the years to witness animal sacrifice, prostitution, or, on some ancient occasions, child sacrifice to the god Pan. In Jesus' day, if there were gates to hell, it was in Caesarea Philippi.

It's here that Jesus tells Peter that Peter's knowledge of Jesus' identity was the rock on which Jesus would build his church... and get this, "the gates of hell will not prevail against it."

Jesus tells us that he is going to build the church in such a way that the gates of hell, the very place where lives are thrown away and creation wasted, will not overcome the church.

What would it look like for the church to become a force in the world that works against the gates of hell of our day... a regenerating force against the needless waste and sacrifice of money, land, resources, and community opportunities? What if Christians, not only individually, but the people of God corporately took this call seriously? What would it look like for the hells of waste not to prevail against the church today?

How can we embody hope in the world like this? To change this narrative, the church must be about leveraging our resources in regenerative and hope giving ways. The amount of land and buildings that the church possesses worldwide is massive. The Catholic Church alone, worldwide, owns 177 million acres of land, second in the world only to Queen Elizabeth herself![2]

Imagine if the Christian church collectively began worldwide initiatives to make these spaces holy ground, land set-apart for the reconciling work of God? What would it look like that every church facility received energy audits and became more energy efficient in our places of worship? And what if we took that saved money and weatherized the homes of the poor and elderly of our community? What if wherever there was a local church there was a refuge for those needing to reconnect with creation? What if churches were known to be places where trees were planted, where fruit grew on the vine ready to be picked, where there was a "big big table with lots and lots of food and a big big yard where we can play football?"[3] What might it look like that we become better stewards of all these places, and that they were known to be good news for the whole community?

One question we've continually tried to ask ourselves as a local church is: *"If we suddenly disappeared from our community today, who would notice or care?"* Asking this regularly can prove to be eye-opening! Wasting our opportunity in time and space to preach the good news and embody the love of

Christ to the communities in which our church buildings re-
side might be the biggest waste of all.

What if every faith community that owned land became less
interested in mowing grass and more interested in food for-
esting? What if churches around the world became places of
food refuge where there was always something good to eat?
What if the Garden of Eden became a blueprint for our spaces
of worship? What if stewarding the ground in this way actually *is* a means of worship?

What if we re-entered the waste-less cycle of God's creative
action?

Re-entering the Circle

"One of our names for Nature is Mother Nature, and this
surely is not because of her partiality for individuals among
her children, but rather because, like a thrifty housewife, she
wastes nothing, not a bite of food or a drop of water. She
keeps serving a menu of delectable and nourishing leftovers."
- **Wendell Berry** [4]

My favorite season is autumn. When summer finally gives
way to that first cool breeze, and the pumpkins come into
harvest, and the leaves change colors, that's what's up! The
fall is a season that reminds us of the death to life pattern of
creation. Leaves fall from trees giving nutrients to the grass,
animals eat the grass, eventually dying and returning to the

ground, then creating more healthy soil for more vegetation, and on and on and on.

Creation, as God intended, is circular.

It endlessly moves forward and grows and matures, meanwhile not a single seed or grain is wasted.

Today, we as humanity must relearn how to be circular like creation is designed to be. When humanity exits this eternally renewable circle of the natural world, the entire ecosystem of our planet begins to tilt off balance. Imagine a scale where one side keeps getting piled higher than the other. Eventually the entire scale will fall over.

We are living in the moment before the scale collapses.

To quote a great moment from a great movie:
"You have forgotten who you are and so have forgotten me. Look inside yourself... You are more than what you have become. You must take your place in the Circle of Life." - The Lion King [5] (Because sometimes you just have to quote something James Earl Jones says.)

Earlier we took note that *when* God creates, there is no waste, and even further that *what* God creates mimics this no-waste pattern. Creation is naturally efficient. The natural world left to its devices is circular in a self-regenerating manner.

What does it mean for us to step back inside the circle?

It sounds overly simplistic because in some ways it is that simple.

How can we, once again, find ourselves at one with the natural world, as God created us to be?

The wonderful news about all this is, these aren't lofty ideals that we can hopefully get to one day... but there are real places in the world where people, companies, and economies are already operating in this circular pattern!

In a corner of the world you may not have looked before, on the northwestern side of an island of Denmark, lies a Danish city of about 16,000 people, called Kalundborg. Kalundborg is home to a model of environmental sustainability that companies around the globe are learning from. Here lies the first industrial symbiosis in the world, called the Kalundborg Symbiosis.[6]

This is a unique partnership that exists between 11 companies along with the municipality of Kalundborg, that produces no waste! Each of these industrial plants uses one another's refuse in their manufacturing process. From a pharmaceutical and enzyme manufacturing plant to an oil refinery, these companies reuse, recycle, and refurbish each other's byproducts of water, energy or materials to make their "new" product. The residue of one place becomes the recourse of the other in an endless loop that benefits not only the environment but the economy. Perhaps what is most surprising about this partnership is that it didn't begin for environmental reasons, it began for economic purposes! Even though the Symbiosis reduces carbon dioxide emissions by 635,000 metric tons a year, it also saves the companies involved $27 million annually. This right here is a story of hope for us today! [7] [8]

What's happening in Kalundborg is an example of an economic system that aims at eliminating all waste, pollution, and carbon emissions through reusing and recycling all resources involved. This is called a circular economy. This reusing and sharing of resources creates a closed loop system in which no new material needs to be put into it to achieve production, and no old material needs to be discarded. Every output from one business should become the food for another. [9]

What I love about what's happening in Denmark is that it's an actual real model of how we can re-enter this natural cycle we were created for. You may not own your own company or be in charge of a big business, or much of anything really, but what you do possess, what you are in control of matters just as much. And you are the only one with your life, you are the doorkeeper of your own choices. What are the ways you can step into a symbiosis with others in your own life? What output might be your neighbor's input?

It is not simply people in powerful places who will change the world. It is you. It is about each of us taking steps toward re-generative justice and actions to re-enter into the sort of economy that is life giving for everyone and everything involved.

In Kent, Washington, Hillside Church of the Nazarene in partnership with World Relief has taken this connection between loving God, loving neighbor, and loving the Earth to the next level. This is one of the most diverse cities in the United States. Kent has a large and growing population of refugees, but they mostly had no place to grow their own culturally appropriate food. Seeing this need, people from the church and World Relief joined hands, picked up tools, and amazingly began the work of de-paving parking lots and turning them into gardens! This difficult and beautiful work gave way to what is now Hillside Paradise Parking Plots Community Garden! Today this is the largest green water site in Washington, with five rain gardens capturing around 3,000 gallons a year. These now lush plots of land help feed refugee families, have created rich soil and community, and are seeing heaven breaking in daily! [10]

Stories like that in Kent, Washington give us hope and stir our creative imaginations of what is possible!

The kind of service communities of faith must engage in may or may not get headlines. The sort of work we're called to do in the cities and communities which we live in may involve handling the trash, it may involve cleaning the baseboards, it may involve deconstructing the pavement of yesterday. The challenge is that we would engage in the work of re-creating the places around us. The clergy of tomorrow must have a Bible in one hand and a garden trowel in the other. God's people must become advocates of health, better living, and thriving community life because ultimately, we are about faithfully stewarding what is already in our care.

For too long we've only been about rescuing those from drowning by pulling person after person out of the river. But the church must now begin the journey upstream to reconcile God's people with God's planet, thus beginning the work of ark building and creation saving.

What would it say that the people who kept our neighborhood streets clean were the church?
What would it say that those who took care of community recycling was the church?
What might it communicate to the world that the ones who were finding a way forward amidst the waste crisis of our day were the people of God?
What if the local church were the ones regenerating biodiversity and topsoil in homes and yards and fields of all their people?
What if the people of God were the first ones grabbing the hands of their neighbors in solidarity and protest of environmental injustices?

What if every local church was known for its kingdom local action?

What if the local church around the world were seed sowers of circular economies? What if this is what it really means to have "all things in common?"[11]

What if so much of this work is just about returning to that moment in Acts when the people of God were filled with the Spirit?

I wonder if the local church today has lost much of its voice to the multitudes because it has lost its relevance to the meager. We want to speak into large issues of life and death but are frequently absent in conversations around the impact of waste on vulnerable communities, the erosion of our topsoil, the lungs of our children, and the poverty along our streets. Until we are faithful in tending to the Earth, we'll never have the authority nor context to truly care for the lives from which grow from it. Until we are faithful with the little things, with loving in local ways, in the parts-per-million, in particulate matter, with the microbiome, with biodiversity, with what's under the trash-lid, we'll never have a rapport with more.

> "Be faithful in small things because it is in them that your strength lies."
> - **Mother Teresa**

Ultimately, we all stand guard at different doors and different intersections. We each have a special part of the garden that we are called to serve and keep. The hard thing will always be to resist what society has deemed "acceptable" from entering and taking root in our part of the garden. We also must go to work to clean up the waste polluting our allotment. Rooting out the weeds of waste is a job each of us is responsible for in whatever ways we have the power and position to contribute to this planetary team effort. Embodying the kingdom of God on Earth will always involve intentionality. The question is, will we be a people known for how comfortable we were in the face of global environmental degradation? Or will each one of us choose to stand our ground against the principalities and gods of excess today?

Respond & Reflect

Respond

→ *Find your next steps toward eliminating waste in your area.*

Visit EcocycleSolutionsHub.org to discover tools to get started eliminating waste in your community!

→ *Take a personal inventory of the places where you are a "doorkeeper."*

This could be as far reaching as an opportunity to create a company-wide green team initiative or simply reassessing the products you use to wash your hair!
What are three things you already have the power to do right now that could begin making a difference?

Record the ways you are beginning to engage in this work! Tag your progress! #GarbageTheologyBook

→ *The Take Action Tool*

How might the people of God become political kingdom advocates for the Earth? Politics are about the way we do life together: how we eat, the water we drink, the ways we travel, our health, and everything in between! The kingdom of heaven is about a certain kind of polity. It is about a polity of love; it is a polity that gives life to everyone present. In order for us to make a difference today and be a regenerative presence in a world that is wasting away, we must be involved in advocating for holistic kingdom-like policies.

We've spent a good deal of time discussing change from the "bottom up," but we must also be people who work, as much as possible, from the "top down." When was the last time you called your Senator? When was the last time you wrote your District Representative? When was the last time you marched? In a democracy, voting and political engagement means that we can pray "your kingdom come" with our lives. Not to say that your nation and religion should ever be one and the same, but to declare that *in every way and effort* that we can promote loving God, loving our neighbor, and loving the Earth... we should most certainly be about it. How might we become political advocates of a gospel that proclaims there is no waste, only misappropriated creation?

Visit the Evangelical Environmental Network's website – CreationCare.org and go to "Get Involved" → "Take Action" and there you'll find connecting with your State Senators and Representatives around issues of creation justice is made easy!

Call or write a letter to your representative and let them know how important it is to you to care for our common home through environmental policies. *(These actions are so important and do make a difference!)*

→ *Pursue an Energy Study for your place of worship.*

What if you could double your missions giving? The church tends to spend exponentially more annually on energy and facility maintenance than we do missions. Prestonwood Baptist Church in Plano, Texas, is a great example of how congregations can successfully lower their facility's energy use. They were able to cut their energy use by 33 percent while lowering their annual energy cost by $725,000! Not only that, but they are saving 10.5 million pounds of CO_2 from entering the atmosphere. In 2007, Prestonwood Baptist Church won the 2007 Energy Star Award for Small Businesses and Congregations. [12]

Why shouldn't we all be able to share such great news?

Visit type in "Energy Star for Congregations" and you will find a great online resource for pursuing energy efficiency for your church.
www.energystar.gov/buildings/owners_and_managers/congregations

Reflect

It has been said that the local church is the hope of the world. The kingdom of God always comes relationally through real people in real places, locally. Our ecclesial calling involves holy resources and particular people, places, and things.

How might the local church today reconnect the good news with everything the church possesses?

How might we be better stewards of our facilities in order to embody good news to our local communities?

How might the church embody a circular ecclesiology where we live out an Acts 2 sharing of resources with all those around us?

What if the local church was the first place people looked to see what a regenerative vision of the future looked like?

Would your church consider investing in solar panels? In green roofs? In creating a community garden? In planting fruit trees? Name some ways you believe the local church could embody hope for creation today.

CHAPTER ELEVEN

Eschatologically Present

12.9.15

December 9th, 2015, at about 2:30 in the afternoon I was parked at a dumpster in East Nashville unloading everything from the back of my truck. Something I had done a thousand times… yet this time would be life changing. On this day, a quarter-inch thick, three by six-foot, glass tabletop lay there ready to be unloaded. I had handled large pieces of glass many times before, but it only takes one bad move with glass for it to go wrong. It's kind of how we never give two-seconds thought to driving 70 miles per hour a few feet away from other cars all the time. As I began sliding the glass out of the rear of the truck, I hadn't paid much attention to the fact that one side was already slightly cracked. I went on half-way picking up and half-way sliding the large piece out, but before I knew what happened, one corner had slightly hit the metal dumpster. It was at that moment that everything dramatically changed. The glass had sliced into my wrist and hand.

I don't remember feeling any pain at all. Before it had even registered in my brain what had happened, I felt such a warmness running down my body. I looked down to discover it was blood. It was at that moment that the panic set in. I looked around for help, but there was no-one around. This place is crawling with people on most days, but on this particular day there was hardly a person there. My phone was in the truck, not that that would have mattered much if I'd had it because my right wrist was severely cut and my left hand had the grip of life over the injury, holding it as tight as I could muster with my work gloves still on. Down the hill I noticed one of the convenience center workers and I yelled at him to call for help. Of course, he didn't have a phone either! At this point my thoughts were of my family, my wife who was 9 months pregnant, and our two-year-old little girl. Then I had the haunting thought that this garbage facility might just be the very last place I visit in my life, and the last thing I'll have been doing is hauling trash.

A few moments later another man pulled up in his truck and called 911 for me. Emergency responders came, and as you might have guessed, I'm very much alive today. As it turns out, I severed four tendons, two nerves, and an artery. After hand surgery to repair the damage and sixteen weeks of hand therapy, I can mostly move my hand around like normal, save the ability to feel the right side of my hand or spread my fingers in an outward motion.

Each one of our lives can change in a moment. We've always heard that, but it's close to impossible to understand unless you've experienced a close call. Until something wakes you up personally, it's hard to be awake. No one wants to have a near death experience. No one wants to lose a loved one. No one wants to experience these life shattering moments. Yet the irony is that it is those who make it through difficult times, who return to life with heightened awareness. When the fog clears and the pain begins to subside a little, a new clarity emerges... all of the sudden there's a clearness about the fragility of things and the importance of our lives.

The truth is, a book cannot give you such a moment. I could write endlessly about the ins and outs of the wastefulness occurring in our world, but you might just rather put this book down and go get a snack. Because ultimately:

I can't take you anywhere you don't want to go.

The greatest temptation of our time is to just keep scrolling. When the issues of life get too difficult or vulgar or dark or depressing, we can always just see what else is on. We can change the channel. Honestly, billions of people are doing just that right now.

There is coming a day, without a change in our posture and lifestyle around the care of creation, that will finally wake us all up. The challenge for the people of planet Earth today is that we must wake up before we get woken up by tragedy. If we live our lives in reaction rather than pro-action, we'll have waited too long to prevent the consequences. The risk isn't simply over-run landfills or workers facing unjust situations. Truly, there is an actual de-creating taking place, and creation is groaning more than ever. Because you and I are so connected to this ground we live on, when the relationship becomes this selfish and sinful, the outcomes for us are severe.

The lives of future generations are crying out.
Fresh water is running dry, and topsoil is deteriorating.
The rainforests of the world are disappearing at a rate of 200,000 acres a day.[1]
And we are on the cusp of irreversibly altering the Earth's climate.

I wish I could say to you, "Don't feel alarmed!" But the truth is, the alarm clock is going off. We won't get up any other way. There is a crack in the glass. If we keep unloading this way the whole thing will shatter. If I had known that that crack, that warning, would lead to such an outcome, what would I have done differently? Did I need the injury to wake up? Or would a warning have been enough?

There was a time that I thought my life was being wasted. Especially in the moment everything flashed before my eyes in the middle of a trash facility. Questions came like a flood, "What am I doing here? Have I wasted my life hauling trash? Could there be a worse place to die?"

Later I came to understand that this is the challenge for us all. To see at a deeper level the work we are doing. To see heaven breaking in through our work, particularly in our connection with all materiality. To move from the fear that you are wasting your life, to the faith of willingly losing your life to find it as you follow the Creator. To move from feeling like trash to reaching down and breathing life into the parts of the world laid waste, in the name of Jesus.

There is a permanent mark on my arm, a scar. It is a reminder of what I've already given much of my life to. My hope is that we can all find perspective without the need for more wounds. My prayer is that the warning will be enough.

The End Times

Take the thousand and give it to the one who risked the most. And get rid of this "play-it-safe" who won't go out on a limb. Throw him out into utter darkness.

  – **Matthew 25: 28-30** MSG 2

If I had a dollar for every time someone told me that we were living in the end times, I'd be as wealthy as a TV evangelist! Tragically, what prompts so many believers to declare that "we are near the end" are the very things that should prompt us into loving action. Until we as the people of God do less shoulder-shrugging and looking to the sky and more planting with our hands in the dirt, we will actually miss Jesus' entire warning to "be ready."

I do believe we are living in the end times.

We are near the end of how far our greed and over-consumption can take us without destroying ourselves.

We are near the end of how much we can extract from the Earth without ourselves becoming extracted.

We are at the edge of how much we can throw away before we throw ourselves away.

This is the end times.

It is the end times for unsustainable development.

It is the end times for land degradation we call modern industrial agriculture.

It is the end times for how long we can leverage the lives of our brothers and sisters and planet for our own business-as-usual.

Creation is arriving at its breaking point trying to meet the demands of our wasteful lifestyles.

This is the end.

Reconciliation

For the creation waits with eager longing for the revealing of the children of God; for the creation was subjected to futility, not of its own will but by the will of the one who subjected it, in hope that the creation itself will be set free from its

bondage to decay and will obtain the freedom of the glory of the children of God.
- **Romans 8:19-21**

How is it that so many followers of Jesus seem more captivated with the prospect of escaping life rather than creating life? A generation of believers fearful of being "left behind" have left behind the mission Jesus gave us here on Earth to do.

If your beliefs about God don't call you to loving action in caring for God's creation, then you may be missing something.

If your theology doesn't beckon you to be shaped more into the image of a loving Creator who cares for all he has made, then you may be missing something.

If the evil that seems to advance in the world causes you to consider escaping it more than extending loving hands toward it, you may be missing something.

If your beliefs about the return of Jesus the Christ here on Earth don't involve the active participation of the restoration of all things, then you may be missing something.

If you find yourself more eager for those doing evil to be judged than you are eager to love those who've lost their way, you may be missing something.

If your life as a Jesus follower isn't moving you to embrace the contagious, befriend the street-kid, join hands with the prostitute, connect with the thief, or share a meal with people from every walk of life, you're really missing something.

If you are more interested in abundance, success, wealth, and capital than you are the cross, you are definitely missing something.

The life of a person-of-Jesus is a life lived out here... on Earth. Feet on the ground. Arms around the other. Healing the land. Lifting up the poor. Nurturing the soil. Living little in opposition to the beastly oppressive empire that lives so large. Opening our homes to refugees. Removing our slavery footprint. For the believer, for the Jesus follower, for those moved by love in the world, for the holy person, everything is interconnected. The kingdom of heaven awakens us to the interwovenness of all of creation, and our eschatological hope for all humanity and humus is restoration and reconciliation.

Imaginational Hope

I don't think there is hope without imagination. Hope without imagination is passive, and I believe God calls us each into active hope — a hope that acts.

Guilt is a naturally occurring feeling after taking in information about the present state of our world of waste. But we cannot remain there. We must move through guilt to form dreams for tomorrow.

Truth be told, when Emily and I first started becoming more ecologically minded in our lifestyle choices years ago, I was more of the skeptic. Not having very much money it was easy for me to make a case against buying more expensive "ethical" products. Not to mention drinking any milk that wasn't 2% was almost more than this country boy could bear at first! But one of the things I love about my wife is that she never puts her values in the backseat. We decided that our values would determine our lifestyle as much as possible, not our meager incomes. Sometimes even following Jesus into the grocery store is like stepping out of the boat onto the water. After years of altering our life decisions toward caring for the Earth, we are living better than ever, and I would never go back. We eat better, are healthier, are more connected with the soil and our community, and are loving it.

Sometimes when we think about going green, changing our lifestyles and consumption habits, it doesn't sound fun at all. We often imagine that these "green practices" will lead us to a future that sounds like what our grandparents were trying to get away from. We imagine hard days behind a plow, growing our own wheat, and milking cows. Which if you're up for that, more power to you! But since when have our imaginations been so shallow?

Sometimes Christians are guilty of only imagining futures that involve the world burning, bleeding, and locked in battle.

It's time to change that.

How might the people of God be the prophets that remind us of the kind of future we were created for?

It will be a time when humanity will provide for the basic needs of all, not through more factories and mass production, but by a re-posturing around our resources.

The future will be a time when we learn to celebrate the local business again, even while embracing our interconnectedness with every person everywhere.

The future is sturdy, as we stand against flimsy values and manufacturing to demand something solid and repairable in every home.

The future will be clean as we give more attention to planting trees than building smokestacks, and all children, no matter where they live, have clean air to breathe.

The future will be grounded as educational institutions everywhere embrace the necessity of our ecological interconnection and teach us all how to engage the soil once again, to be servants and keepers of the garden.

The future will be abundant and bountiful as we step further into the stewarding relationship, we were created for with all of creation!

There are all kinds of hope. We just have to start dreaming better dreams.

Your turn.

The future will be

_____

_____

_____

_____

The Next Step

The groaning sound of a truck door struggling open summed up many cold days as I stepped out to face a heaping pile of trash in waiting. Some days, especially early on in the job, the seeming insurmountable size of such a mountain of junk would cause a run of anxiousness down into my chest.

How long would this take?
How many loads is this?
What all is underneath there?
Can I do this?

I'll never forget one particular large home in East Nashville that had been lived in by the same family for decades and was now left to be cleaned out. Everything the family wanted to keep had been kept, and everything else had to go. An attic apartment full of exercise equipment, a bed, and so many books... bedrooms and closets full of clothes and church hats, gardening monuments keeping watch over the yard, a shed untouched by a generation, and a basement that would make American Pickers drool. We hauled 21 loads from that house.

The difficult piece is *how* to haul 21 loads. To responsibly deal with each item requires so much thought and intentionality. Some items can be donated, others recycled, antiqued, or sold online. Some items are fat and bulky, some thin, long, sharp, empty, or extremely heavy. To handle all of this material efficiently and fit it piece by piece into an eight-foot truck bed is no small task... perhaps even an art form. [3]

When there is this much waste, where do you even start?

It can be paralyzing as one stares at the size of the task ahead. There is no doubt about that. However, there is something that I learned after years of hauling loads of garbage like these... it's that I'm still here. I'm still breathing. Every one of those insurmountable jobs, I finished. I went home at the end of each day. Where there once was an enormous pile of junk was now a clean lot.

What I learned, quite literally, over thousands of truckloads, was to just pick up the very next thing. The secret is simply picking up one piece of trash at a time. Indeed, there often is no good place to start. We must all begin by just dealing with what is right at our feet, right now, piece by piece.

The issues of waste on our planet today are gargantuan. It is only natural for us to feel overwhelmed by the task ahead. It will take great strides to correct the course of our lives, our consumption habits, and the very posture we take in the world with all materiality. But the path forward has, and always will, begin with just one simple step forward. And the next. Then the next after that.

So the question is, what is your next step?

Maybe for you that involves taking inventory of what is inside your home.

Maybe you need to start in the attic and move room by room to the garage.

Maybe your next step is reworking your home recycling protocols.

Maybe your next step is purchasing slave-free and fair-trade goods.

Maybe your next step is moving beyond your personal space and into your workplace as you go low-waste.

Maybe your next step is investing in a local CSA.

Maybe your next step is starting a non-profit.

Maybe your next step is mobilizing a neighborhood composting coalition.

Maybe you're ready to start your repair café.

Maybe your next step is transforming whatever organization you're already a part of.

Maybe your next step is getting more involved in local politics.

Everyone has a different next step. But what is important is that you take it. Together we will all walk into a healthier and holier tomorrow.

Resurrecting All Things

For in him all the fullness of God was pleased to dwell, and through him God was pleased to reconcile to himself all things, whether on Earth or in heaven, by making peace through the blood of his cross.

- Colossians 1:19-20

In my neighborhood every second Friday the recycling truck comes at the crack of dawn. These recycling workers are true community servants out for long days dealing with our remains. There's been more than one occasion, having forgotten to wheel the cans to the street, I hear the rumbling of the recycle truck and spring from my bed, barefoot and shirtless, to wheel them out! They come early in the morning, and before the fog has lifted, they're out there emptying our bins.

Perhaps like so many other things in our lives these ordinary moments can be divine metaphors for us if we allow them to be. Just like the recycling workers, God comes by early in the morning on the third day, and by the time we get out there to see, the lid is already pulled away and the tomb is empty. To our great shock and amazement, we learn through Jesus' resurrection that death, the great conclusion of waste, has already been transformed!

May these be the connections we make… between Jesus' empty tomb and an empty waste bin. We must see how resurrection is about a reconciling of "all things." Maybe this kind of associating something holy with something that typically feels irreverent (like our garbage) creates a sense of shock. This is how scandalous our salvation story truly is. The bodily resurrection of Jesus on Earth is about the eschatological hope for all creation. Jesus' resurrection from the tomb is a divine telescope for us to see the future resurrection and transformation of all things, not just our bodies.

My hope is that one day soon we will look into the bins lined by the curb and find them all empty.
Empty because the people of God have become more intentional people in the world.
Empty because we are living out of a call unto holiness.
Empty because we have taken a seat in the redemptive work Christ left us to do in the world.
Empty because love is being embodied in the relationship we have with everyone and everything.
Empty because Jesus lives!

We possess the power to choose life. Let us choose the path of resurrection over waste. Let us pray that humanity may be found faithful with every choice we are faced with, no matter the size. We will change the world not in great and awe-inspiring acts or gestures, but we will change this world of waste with millions of microscopic choices. From the words we say, to the farmers we support, to the coffee we drink, to the electronics we purchase, to the clothes we wear, to the gardens we grow, to what we wrap our leftovers in, to actually eating those later on! Because for a people created in the image of a Creator, all matter matters, and every belonging belongs. Holy living is wholly living. Entire is entire. Your salvation is intertwined with the unseen world of waste and the salvation of every person, every place, every thing.

May our lives become our embodied prayers, transforming our world, in the name of the Father, Son, and Holy Spirit. Amen.

The air is cold, but I know the work will warm me up. Reaching onto the dash I search for a right and then a left-handed glove, walking around and opening the passenger door I pull a new trash bag from behind the seat flinging it open into the air. Now, bending over to the ground in front of me, the transformation begins...

Notes

Chapter 1

[1] BBC World News, "Bali's battle against plastic pollution," https://www.bbc.com/news/world-asia-43312464, accessed 23 April 2020

[2] USA TODAY, "World's largest collection of ocean garbage is twice the size of Texas," https://www.usatoday.com/story /tech/science/2018/03/22/great-pacific-garbage-patch-grows/446405002/, accessed 29 April 2018.

[3] NOAA Marine Debris Program – Office of Response and Restoration, "Garbage Patches," https://marinedebris.noaa.gov/ movement/great-pacific-garbage-patch, accessed 23 April 2020

[4] The World Counts, "A World of Waste," https://www.theworld-counts.com/challenges/planet-Earth/state-of-the-planet/world-waste-facts, accessed 25 May 2020

[5] United States Environmental Protection Agency, "National Overview: Facts and Figures on Materials, Wastes and Recycling," https://www.epa.gov/facts-and-figures-about-materials-waste-and-recycling/national-overview-facts-and-figures-materi-als#Landfilling, accessed 25 May 2020

[6] BBC, "A rubbish story: China's mega-dump full 25 years ahead of schedule," https://www.bbc.com/news/world-asia-50429119, accessed 4 June 2020

[7] CNA, "Indonesia's flowing rivers of trash," https://www.chan-nelnewsasia.com/news/cnainsider/indonesia-s-flowing-rivers-of-trash-12665922, accessed 23 April 2020

[8] The World Counts, "We only have one future" https://www.the-worldcounts.com/challenges/planet-Earth/state-of-the-planet/overuse-of-resources-on-Earth, accessed 24 March 2020

[9] The Washington Post, "The world is drowning in ever-growing mounds of garbage," https://www.washingtonpost.com/world/africa/the-world-is-drowning-in-ever-growing-mounds-of-garbage/2017/11/21/cf22e4bd-17a4-473c-89f8-873d48f968cd_story.html?noredirect=on&utm_term=.e4b4d1ed5893, accessed 11 January 2019.

[1] EPA, "Landfill Technical Data," https://www.epa.gov/lmop/landfill-technical-data, accessed 11 May 2020

[2] Fast Company, "These Maps Show How Many Landfills There Are In The U.S.,"_https://www.fastcompany.com/3062853/these-maps-show-how-much-of-the-us-is-covered-in-landfills, accessed 11 May 2020

[3] The Measure of Things, "How heavy is 74,984,000 tons?," https://www.bluebulbprojects.com/measureofthings/results.php?amt=74984000&comp=weight&unit=tns&searchTerm=how+heavy+74984000+tons, accessed 25 May 2020

[4] Green America, "Americans are really bad at recycling. But only because we're not trying very hard." https://www.greenamerica.org/rethinking-recycling/americans-are-really-bad-recycling-only-because-were-not-trying-very-hard, accessed 27 May 2020

[5] Dumpsters.com, "Curbing America's Trash Production: Statistics and Solutions," https://www.dumpsters.com/blog/us-trash-production, accessed 11 May 2020

[6] Business Insider, "Amazon's delivery business reveals staggering growth as it's on track to deliver 3.5 billion packages globally

this year", https://www.businessinsider.com/amazon-package-delivery-business-growth-2019-12, accessed 12 May 2020

[7] "The Parable of the River" has many possible tellings and origins that go back a century, this is my own retelling - People are camped out by a waterfall and begin to see children washing downstream and drowning from the river. They get to work immediately pulling person after person out of the water. Tire and exhausted they work endlessly unable to save every child. Finally, someone has the idea to move upstream to see how these children are falling into the river and solve the crisis.

[8] Consumers International, "Built to fail: is planned obsolescence really happening?," https://www.consumersinternational.org/news-resources/blog/posts/built-to-fail-is-planned-obsolescence-really-happening/, accessed 20 May 2020

[9] Sustainability For All, "The Battle Against Planned Obsolescence," https://www.activesustainability.com/sustainable-development/battle-against-planned-obsolescence/, accessed 20 May 2020

[10] The Story of Stuff Project, "Making Change Together," https://www.storyofstuff.org/, accessed 20 May 2020

[11] Fashionista, "What Really Happens To Your Clothing Donations?," https://fashionista.com/2016/01/clothing-donation, accessed 20 May 2020

[12] Business Insider, "Goodwill stores are filling up with cheap pieces no one wants — and it reveals a huge problem with the way people shop for clothes," https://www.businessinsider.com/goodwill-overrun-with-fast-fashion-donations-2018-2, accessed 20 May 2020

Chapter 2

[1] NASA, "Blue Marble - Image of the Earth from Apollo 17," https://www.nasa.gov/content/blue-marble-image-of-the-Earth-from-apollo-17, accessed 1 June 2020

[2] Global Algae Innovations, http://www.globalgae.com/, accessed 24 April 2020

[3] Genesis 2:4-7 The Voice (VOICE)

The Voice Bible Copyright © 2012 Thomas Nelson, Inc. The Voice™ translation © 2012 Ecclesia Bible Society All rights reserved.

Chapter 3

[1] Matthew 10:7-8 NRSV

[2] "Manifesto: The Mad Farmer Liberation Front" from The Country of Marriage, Harcourt Brace Jovanovich, Inc. 1973. Also published by Counterpoint Press in The Selected Poems of Wendell Berry, 1999; The Mad Farmer Poems, 2008; New Collected Poems, 2012.

[3] BBC, "What would happen if bees went extinct?," https://www.bbc.com/future/article/20140502-what-if-bees-wentextinct#:~:text=We%20may%20lose% 20all%20the, amount%20of%20fruit%20and%20vegetables., Accessed 11 August 2020

[4] Genesis 1:28 NRSV

[5] For in him all the fullness of God was pleased to dwell, and through him God was pleased to reconcile to himself all things, whether on Earth or in heaven, by making peace through the blood of his cross." – Colossians 1:19-20

[6] The Church of the Nazarene is an evangelical Wesleyan-holiness Christian denomination that emerged from the 19th-century Holiness movement in North America.

[7] Church of the Nazarene, MANUAL 2017–2021 - Sacraments and Rituals, Section 705

[8] John 2:1-11

[9] Psalm 24:1

[10] United States Environmental Protection Agency "Facts and Figure about Materials, Waste, and Recycling," https://www.epa.gov/facts-and-figures-about-materials-waste-and-recycling/nondurable-goods-product-specific-data, Accessed 28 January 2020

[11] J. Matthew Sleeth. *Serve God, Save the Planet: A Christian Call to Action.* Zondervan, 2007. Print.

Chapter 4

[1] Ephesians 1:18, New Revised Standard Version

[2] Science Alert, "Electrons Have Been Caught Disappearing And Reappearing Between Atomic Layers," https://www.sciencealert.com/electrons-have-been-caught-disappearing-and-reappearing-between-atomic-layers, accessed 1 June 2020

Chapter 5

[1] Jeremiah 7:31 NRSV

[2] Mark 9:47-48 NRSV

[3] The Rabbit Room, "Is The Name Of God The Sound Of Our Breathing?", https://rabbitroom.com/2011/08/is-the-name-of-god-the-sound-of-our-breathing, accessed 22 October 2020

[4] Centers for Disease Control and Prevention, "Particle Pollution," https://www.cdc.gov/air/particulate_matter.html, accessed 10 June 2020

[5] Communities for A Better Environment, https://www.cbe-cal.org/, accessed 11 June 2020

[6] Particle Matter 2.5 (PM 2.5) Are fine inhalable particles, with diameters that are generally 2.5 micrometers and smaller.

[7] Parts per million (PPM) is the number of units of mass of a contaminant per million units of total mass.

[8] Patagonia, "District 15 | Communities for a Better Environment," Film, https://www.patagonia.com/activism/, accessed 10 June 2020

[9] GlobalChange.gov, Climate and Health Assessment, Chapter 9, https://health2016.globalchange.gov/populations-concern, accessed 13 August 2020

[10] Children's Environmental Health Network, "Reports and Publications," https://cehn.org/our-work/research/, accessed 8 June 2020

[11] Bruce Bekkar, MD; Susan Pacheco, MD; Rupa Basu, PhD, et al; "Association of Air Pollution and Heat Exposure With Preterm Birth, Low Birth Weight, and Stillbirth in the US - A Systematic Review," https://jamanetwork.com/journals/jamanetworkopen/fullarticle/2767260?utm_source=For_The_Media&utm_medium=referral&utm_campaign=ftm_links&utm_term=061820, 28 July 2020

[12] Liuhua Shi, Xiao Wu, Mahdieh Danesh Yazdi, Danielle Braun, Yara Abu Awad, Yaguang Wei, Pengfei Liu, Qian Di, Yun Wang, Joel Schwartz, Francesca Dominici, Marianthi-Anna Kioumourtzoglou, Antonella Zanobetti (2020) "Long-term effects of PM2.5

on neurological disorders in the American Medicare population: a longitudinal cohort study," The Lancet Planetary Health doi: 10.1016/S2542-5196(20)30227-8

[13] American Lung Association State of the Air, "People at Risk," http://www.stateoftheair.org/key-findings/people-at-risk.html, accessed 28 July 2020

[14] Leonardo Trasande, Patrick Malecha, and Teresa M. Attina, Particulate Matter Exposure and

Preterm Birth: Estimates of U.S. Attributable Burden and Economic Costs, ENVIRONMENTAL HEALTH

PERSPECTIVES, http://dx.doi.org/10.1289/ehp.1510810, July 2020

[15] Global - 9 million deaths in 2015: Landrigan PJ, Fuller R, Acosta NJR, et al. The *Lancet* Commission on pollution and health. *Lancet* 2017, published online Oct 19. http://dx.doi.org /10.1016/S0140-6736(17)32345-0.

[16] ResearchGate, The Lancet Commission on pollution and health, https://www.researchgate.net/publica-tion/320521239_The_Lancet_Commission_on_pollu-tion_and_health, accessed 13 August 2020

[17] microgram per cubic meter (µg/m3)

[18] American Lung Association, "Particle Pollution," https://www.lung.org/clean-air/outdoors/what-makes-air-un-healthy/particle-pollution, accessed 10 June 2020

[19] U.S. EPA. Integrated Science Assessment for Particulate Matter, December 2019. EPA/600/R-19/188. https://cfpub.epa.gov/ncea/isa/recordisplay.cfm?deid=347534

[20] Skeptical Science, "Breaking News...The Earth is Warming... Still. A LOT," https://www.skepticalscience.com/ Breaking

News_ The_Earth_is_Warming_Still_A_LOT.html, accessed 25 June 2020

[21] Climate Scientist Katherine Hayhoe, "What's the Big Deal With a Few Degrees? | Global Weirding," https://www.youtube.com/watch?v=6cRCbgTA_78, accessed 11 June 2020

[22] SkepticalScience, "Global weirding with Katharine Hayhoe: Natural Cycles," https://www.skepticalscience.com/global-weirding-not-natural-cycle.html, accessed 7 August 2020

[23] Climate.gov, "Climate Change: Atmospheric Carbon Dioxide," https://www.climate.gov/news-features/understanding-climate/climate-change-atmospheric-carbon-dioxide, accessed 25 June 2020

[24] International Panel on Climate Change, "Special Report Global Warming of 1.5 ºC," https://www.ipcc.ch/sr15/, accessed 11 June 2020

[25] Climate.gov, "Climate Change: Global Temperature," https://www.climate.gov/news-features/understanding-climate/climate-change-global-temperature, accessed 12 June 2020

[26] Katherine Hayhoe - Climate Scientist, "THE RESPONSE TO CLIMATE CHANGE COMES FROM THE HEART," http://www.katharinehayhoe.com/wp2016/2016/05/08/the-response-to-climate-change-comes-from-the-heart/, accessed 12 June 2020

[27] United States Environmental Protection Agency, "Climate Change Indicators in the United States," https://www.epa.gov/climate-indicators, accessed 12 June 2020

28   PPIC,   "California's   Latest   Drought,"
https://www.ppic.org/publication/californias-latest-drought/,
accessed 6 August 2020

29 National Geographic, "Europe has had five 500-year summers
in 15 years. And now this."   https://www.nationalgeo-
graphic.com/environment/2019/06/europe-has-had-five-500-
year-summers-in-15-years/#close, accessed 7 August 2020

30   CDC,   "Climate   Heath   -   Temperature   Extremes,"
https://www.cdc.gov/climateandhealth/effects/tempera-
ture_extremes.htm, accessed 6 August 2020

31 World Health Organization, "Heatwaves," https://
www.who .int/health-topics/heatwaves#tab=tab_1, accessed 6
August 2020 32 Nunn, P.D., Kohler, A. & Kumar, R. "Identifying and
Assessing Evidence for Recent Shoreline Change Attributable To
Uncom-monly Rapid Sea-Level Rise in Pohnpei, Federated State of
Micro-nesia, Northwest Pacific Ocean." Journal of Coast
Conservation (2017) 21: 719. https://doi.org/10.1007/
s11852-017-0531-7 33 The Guardian, "'One day we'll disappear':
Tuvalu's sinking is-lands,"   https://www.theguardian.com/
global-development /2019/may/16/one-day-disappear-tuvalu-
sinking-islands-rising-seas-climate-change, accessed 7 August
2020

34 Forbes, "New Study Finds 8 Islands Swallowed By Rising Sea
Level,"   https://www.forbes.com/sites/trevornace/2017/
09/09/new-study-finds-8-islands-swallowed-by-rising-sea-level/
#122e34025283, accessed 10 August 2020

35 Brookings, "The climate crisis, migration, and refugees,"
https://www.brookings.edu/research/the-climate-crisis-migra-
tion-and-refugees/, accessed 7 August 2020

[36] Kumari Rigaud, Kanta, Alex de Sherbinin, Bryan Jones, Jonas Bergmann, Viviane Clement, Kayly Ober, Jacob Schewe, Susana Adamo, Brent McCusker, Silke Heuser, and Amelia Midgley. 2018. Groundswell: Preparing for Internal Climate Migration. The World Bank. Pg 2. https://openknowledge.worldbank.org/handle/10986/29461

[37] Cook, J., Supran, G., Lewandowsky, S., Oreskes, N., & Maibach, E., (2019). America Misled:

How the fossil fuel industry deliberately misled Americans about climate change.

Fairfax, VA: George Mason University Center for Climate Change Communication.

Available at https://www.climatechangecommunication.org/america-misled/

[38] John Wesley. Sermon 51 - The Good Steward. Edited by Kristina Hedstrom, student at Northwest Nazarene College (Nampa, ID), with corrections by George Lyons for the Wesley Center for Applied Theology. Accessed 10 August 2020. http://www.wbbm.org/john-wesley-sermons/serm-051.htm.

Chapter 6

[1] See Leviticus 25:8-55 for the Year of Jubilee

[2] Inequality.org, "Wealth Inequality in the United States," https://inequality.org/facts/wealth-inequality/, accessed 4 Januaury 2021

[3] Kunzig, Robert. "The End of Waste." *National Geographic,* Mar. 2020, pp. 42-71

[4] United Methodist Insight, "Environmentalist: Humans Are 'Running Genesis in Reverse.'" https://um-insight.net/in-the-

world/disasters-and-climate-change/environmentalist-humans-are-running-genesis-in-reverse/, accessed 8 July 2020

[5] McKibben, Bill. Eaarth: Making a Life on a Tough New Planet. New York: Times Books, 2010. Print.

[6] PNAS, "The biomass distribution on Earth," https://www.pnas.org/content/115/25/6506, accessed 9 July 2020

[7] The Proceedings of the National Academy of Sciences (PNAS), "Vertebrates on the brink as indicators of biological annihilation and the sixth mass extinction" https://www.pnas.org/content/117/24/13596#:~:text=The%20ongoing%20sixth%20mass%20species,the%20degradation%20of%20ecosystem%20services., accessed 30 December 2020

[8] Pyschguides.com, "Shopping Addiction Symptoms, Causes and Effects," https://www.psychguides.com/behavioral-disorders/shopping/addiction/#:~:text=According%20to%20Ruth%20Engs%20from,time%2C%20these%20feelings%20become%20addictive., accessed 21 January 2020

[9] Luke 15:29-31

[10] Matthew 5:38-48

[11] Genesis 1:26

Chapter 7

[1] The World Counts, "Slavery still exists?" https://www.theworldcounts.com/stories/Modern_Day_Slavery_Statistics, accessed 24 March 2020

[2] Bales, Kevin. Blood and Earth: Modern Slavery, Ecocide, and the Secret to Saving the World. New York: Spiegel & Grau, 2016. Print.

[3] KGOU, Why Modern-Day Slavery Is A Drag On The Economy And Environment," https://www.kgou.org/post/why-modern-day-slavery-drag-economy-and-environment, accessed 5 November 2020

[4] Bales, Kevin. *Blood and Earth: Modern Slavery, Ecocide, and the Secret to Saving the World.* Page 10. New York: Spiegel & Grau, 2016. Print.

[5] Reuters, "Links between slavery, environmental damage are cause for hope, author argues," https://www.reuters.com/article/us-global-trafficking-environment/links-between-slavery-environmental-damage-are-cause-for-hope-author-argues-idUSKCN0UY2TG, accessed 10 August 2020

[6] Yet it is also not so black and white as companies still produce our essential items in ways that are designed for the dump. We struggle when that item we need for our livelihood has blood on it, but we need it to go to work every day. When the evils of slavery are still at large in the "great" companies and corporations of today and are not opposed by our actions and policies, the people of God still have some work to do!

[7] The World Counts, https://www.theworldcounts.com, accessed 24 March 2020

[8] John Wesley. Sermon 98 - On Visiting the Sick. Edited by Chris Dinter with corrections by Ryan Danker and George Lyons for the Wesley Center for Applied Theology at Northwest Nazarene University. Accessed 21 June 2021. http://wesley.nnu.edu/john-wesley/the-sermons-of-john-wesley-1872-edition/sermon-98-on-visiting-the-sick/

[9] A fence line community is a neighborhood that is immediately adjacent to a company and is directly affected by the noise, odors,

chemical emissions, traffic, parking, and operations of the company. https://en.wikipedia.org/wiki/Fenceline_community, accessed 2 December 2020

[10] "Inequity in consumption of goods and services adds to racial–ethnic disparities in air pollution

exposure," Christopher W. Tessum, Joshua S. Apte, Andrew L. Goodkind, Nicholas Z. Muller, Kimberley A.

Mullins, David A. Paolella, Stephen Polasky, Nathaniel P. Springer, Sumil K. Thakrar, Julian D.

Marshall, and Jason D. Hill, PNAS March 26, 2019, 116 (13) 6001-6006; first published March 11,

2019 https://doi.org/10.1073/pnas.1818859116

[11] Environmental Law Institute, "An Ongoing Battle: Fighting the Impacts of Uranium Mining in Southwestern Indigenous Communities," https://www.eli.org/vibrant-environment-blog/ongoing-battle-fighting-impacts-uranium-mining-southwestern-indigenous-communities, accessed February 4, 2021

[12] "Redlining is the systematic denial of various services or goods by federal government agencies, local governments, or the private sector either directly or through the selective raising of prices." - https://en.wikipedia.org/wiki/Redlining

[13] Bridge Michigan, "Michigan's segregated past – and present (Told in nine interactive maps)," https://www.bridgemi.com/michigan-government/michigans-segregated-past-and-present-told-9-interactive-maps, accessed 27 January 2021

[14] The Verge, "How the Flint River got so toxic," https://www.theverge.com/2016/2/26/11117022/flint-michigan-water-crisis-lead-pollution-history, accessed 4 January 2021

[15] Lumen Learning, "Environmental Racism" https://courses. lumenlearning.com/alamo-sociology/chapter/reading-environmental-racism/, accessed 26 March 26, 2020

[16] Talk Poverty, "Environmental Racism Is Killing Black Communities In Louisiana," https://talkpoverty.org/2020/01/09/environmental-racism-black-communities-louisiana/, accessed 26 March 2020

[17] University Network for Human Rights, "Waiting to Die: Toxic Emissions and Disease Near the Louisiana Denka/DuPont Plant," https://www.humanrightsnetwork.org/waiting-to-die, accessed 26 March 2020

[18] CNN, "China: The electronic wastebasket of the world," https://www.cnn.com/2013/05/30/world/asia/china-electronic-waste-e-waste/index.html, accessed 26 March 2020

[19] STeP, "What is e-waste?", http://www.step-initiative.org/e-waste-challenge.html accessed 26 March 2020

[20] Climate Institute, "E-waste and how to reduce it", https://climate.org/e-waste-and-how-to-reduce-it/, accessed 26 March 2020

[21] The Guardian, "'Asthma alley': why minorities bear burden of pollution inequity caused by white people," https://www.theguardian.com/us-news/2019/apr/04/new-york-south-bronx-minorities-pollution-inequity, accessed 30 March 2020

[22] NRDC, "Port Arthur, Texas: American Sacrifice Zone," https://www.nrdc.org/onEarth/port-arthur-texas-american-sacrifice-zone, accessed 30 March 2020

[23] Climate Analytics, "Black Lives Matter: the link between climate change and racial justice," https://climateanalytics.org

/blog/2020/black-lives-matter-the-link-between-climate-change-and-racial-justice/, accessed 1 September 2020

24 The Nation, "Why #BlackLivesMatter Should Transform the Climate Debate," https://www.thenation.com/article/archive/what-does-blacklivesmatter-have-do-climate-change/, accessed 1 September 2020

25 Malachi 3:5 NRSV

26 John Wesley. Sermon 51 - The Good Steward. Edited by Kristina Hedstrom, student at Northwest Nazarene College (Nampa, ID), with corrections by George Lyons for the Wesley Center for Applied Theology. Accessed 13 August 2020. http://www.wbbm.org/john-wesley-sermons/serm-051.htm. 27 The True Cost, Dir. Andrew Morgan. Untold Creative, 2015. Film.

Chapter 8

1 The True Cost, Dir. Andrew Morgan. Untold Creative, 2015. Film.

1 See Job 38 - 41

2 CAMERON, J., et al. (2010). *Avatar*. Beverly Hills, Calif, 20th Century Fox.

3 KonMari, "Letting Go With Gratitude," https://konmari.com/marie-kondo-gratitude/, accessed 17 June 2020

4 Exodus 16:17-21 NRSV

5 Healthline, "How Long Can You Go Without Sleep? Function, Hallucination, and More" https://www.healthline.com/health/healthy-sleep/how-long-can-you-go-without-sleep, accessed 1 December 2020

Chapter 9

[1] Desertification is the process by which fertile land becomes desert-like, typically as a result of drought, deforestation, or inappropriate agriculture.

[2] Everyone should watch the documentary "Kiss the Ground" to learn more about what is happening to our topsoil around the world. More info found at https://kisstheground.com/

[3] BBC, "Why soil is disappearing from farms," http://www.bbc.com/future/bespoke/follow-the-food/why-soil-is-disappearing-from-farms/, accessed 19 March 2020

[4] Global Agriculture, "Soil Fertility and Erosion," https://www.globalagriculture.org/report-topics/soil-fertility-and-erosion.html, accessed 18 August 2020

[5] Borrelli P, Robinson DA, Fleischer LR, et al. An assessment of the global impact of 21st century land use change on soil erosion. Nat Commun. 2017;8(1):2013. Published 2017 Dec 8. doi:10.1038/s41467-017-02142-7

[6] Farm Progress, "Economics of Soil Loss," https://www.farm-progress.com/soil-health/economics-soil-loss, accessed 4 September 2020

[7] Scientific American, "Only 60 Years of Farming Left If Soil Degradation Continues," https://www.scientificamerican.com/article/only-60-years-of-farming-left-if-soil-degradation-continues, accessed 19 March 2020

[8] Berry, W. (1977). *The unsettling of America: Culture & agriculture*. Berkeley: Counterpoint.

[9] Kuhn, Judy, "Colors of the Wind." Pocahontas Original Soundtrack, Produced by Stephen Schwartz & Alan Menken, Walt Disney Records, 1995, Track 11

[10] Permaculture Principles, "Permaculture Ethics." https://permacultureprinciples.com/ethics/, accessed 21 May 2020

[11] RESET, "Global Food Waste and its Environmental Impact." https://en.reset.org/knowledge/global-food-waste-and-its-environmental-impact-09122018, accessed 19 March 2020

[12] U.S. Food and Drug Administration, "Food Waste and Loss," https://www.fda.gov/food/consumers/food-waste-and-loss , accessed 2 March 2020.

[13] The New York Times, "Dumped Milk, Smashed Eggs, Plowed Vegetables: Food Waste of the Pandemic." https://www.nytimes.com/2020/04/11/business/coronavirus-destroying-food.html, accessed 21 May 2020

[14] The New York Times, "Meat Plant Closures Mean Pigs Are Gassed or Shot Instead." https://www.nytimes.com/2020/05/14/business/coronavirus-farmers-killing-pigs.html?campaign_id=9&emc=edit_nn_20200514&instance_id=18463&nl=the-morning&regi_id=106121136&segment_id=27760&te=1&user_id=9e9722755d46cd30fe0c44f7be0a8d3b&fbclid=IwAR06r-m6svKiSrPMkMWUwAfp0Yndp LSdpDlKK6NVTEvF-FzK0UIO42_LUi8, accessed 21 May 2020

[15] Bales, Kevin. *Blood and Earth: Modern Slavery, Ecocide, and the Secret to Saving the World.* New York: Spiegel & Grau, 2016. Print. – page 213

[16] Smaje, Chris. A Small Farm Future: Making the Case for a Society Built around Local Economies, Self-Provisioning, Agricultural Diversity and a Shared Earth. Chelsea Green Publishing, 2020.

[17] Dumpsters, "These Grocery Store Waste Statistics Are a Wake Up Call," https://www.dumpsters.com/blog/grocery-store-food-waste-statistics, accessed 19 August 2020

[18] Quest, "Food Waste Statistics, The Reality Of Food Waste," https://www.questrmg.com/2019/08/08/food-waste-statistics-the-reality-of-food-waste/, accessed 31 March 2020

[19] OWN, "Lisa Ling Goes on a 'Trash Tour' with Dumpster-Diving Freegans," http://www.oprah.com/own-oprahshow/lisa-ling-goes-on-a-trash-tour-with-dumpster-diving-freegan-video, accessed 27 May 2020

[20] ConstructionDive, "Report: Global construction waste will almost double by 2025," https://www.constructiondive.com/news/report-global-construction-waste-will-almost-double-by-2025/518874/, accessed 31 March 2020

[21] Transparency Market Research, "Construction Waste Management Market - Global Industry Analysis, Size, Share, Trends, Analysis, Growth and Forecast 2018 – 2026," https://www.transparencymarketresearch.com/construction-waste-management-market.html, accessed 31 March 2020

[22] Nashville.gov, "Construction and Demolition Reuse and Recycling", https://www.nashville.gov/Public-Works/Waste-and-Recycling/Construction-and-Demolition-Recycling.aspx, accessed 11 February 2021

[1] Global Agriculture, "Meat and Animal Feed," https://www.globalagriculture.org/report-topics/meat-and-animal-feed.html, accessed 28 July 2020

Chapter 10

[1] The Holy Bible, King James Version. Cambridge Edition: 1769; King James Bible Online, 2021.

[2] Love Money, "Revealed: the world's 101 biggest private landowners,"

https://www.lovemoney.com/gallerylist/70168/revealed-the-worlds-101-biggest-private-landowners, accessed 26 June 2020

3 "Big House" by Audio Adrenaline is still ringing in our ears decades later!

4 The Art of Loading Brush: New Agrarian Writings, by Wendell Berry, Counterpoint, 2017, pp. 211

5 Ferguson, D. (1994). Disney's The Lion King. [United States]: Mouse Works.

6 Symbiosis: a mutually beneficial relationship between different people or groups, often within close proximity

7 Kalundborg Symbiosis, http://www.symbiosis.dk/en/, accessed 20 July 2020

8 Kunzig, Robert. "The End of Waste." *National Geographic,* Mar. 2020, pp. 42-71

9 ELLEN MACARTHUR FOUNDATION, "What Is The Circular Economy?", https://www.ellenmacarthurfoundation.org/circular-economy/what-is-the-circular-economy, accessed 20 July 2020

10 World Relief Seattle, "Paradise Parking Plots Community Garden,"https://worldreliefseattle.org/gaden?fbclid=IwAR3g YQQCA3wP9TfFuhTw8sl2Znlu2Mx_AASidm5aYwXeDYlucDXeuf ZxdnI, accessed 24 April 2020

11 Acts 2:44

12 Energy Star. 2007. In the News: Prestonwood Baptist Church. 2007 Energy Star Award for Small Businesses and Congregations, U.S. Environmental Protection Agency, U.S. Department of Energy, https://archive.epa.gov/epapages/newsroom_archive/news-releases/e7b88caa267b361985257354005232fb.html

Chapter 11

[1] Rain-Tree Publishers, "About the Rainforests," https://rain-tree.com/facts.htm, accessed 18 June 2020

[2] Matthew 25: 28-30, <u>The Message</u> **(MSG)** Copyright © 1993, 2002, 2018 by <u>Eugene H. Peterson</u>

[3] Wendell Berry says it best! "Every piece, every scrap conferred upon the whole load the happiness of its right placement." - The Art of Loading Brush: New Agrarian Writings, by Wendell Berry, Counterpoint, 2017, p. 254

Germinations

[1] CCN, "You could be swallowing a credit card's weight in plastic every week," https://www.cnn.com/2019/06/11/health/microplastics-ingestion-wwf-study-scn-intl/index.html, accessed 25 August 2020

[2] Reuse This Bag, "The Impact of Plastic On the Earth [INFOGRAPHIC]," https://www.reusethisbag.com/articles/the-truth-about-plastic/, accessed 8 June 2020

[3] State of the Planet, "The Truth About Bioplastics," https://blogs.ei.columbia.edu/2017/12/13/the-truth-about-bioplastics/, accessed 12 May 2020

[4] Upstream, "Throw-Away-Free-Places," https://www.upstream-solutions.org/blogs/throw-away-free-places-launch-in-2019, accessed 13 May 2020

[5] DTR - Define The Relationship. Come on, you knew that one!

[6] NRDC, "Wasted: How America Is Losing Up to 40 Percent of Its Food from Farm to Fork to Landfill," https://www.nrdc.org

/resources/wasted-how-america-losing-40-percent-its-food-farm-fork-landfill, accessed 11 Febraury 2021

[7] The Kansas City Star, *How one city turns human waste into compost for your garden,* https://www.kansascity.com/news/nation-world/article144587659.html, accessed March 16, 2020

[8] The Columbian, "Recompose, the first human-composting funeral home in the U.S., is now open for business," https://www.columbian.com/news/2021/jan/24/recompose-the-first-human-composting-funeral-home-in-the-u-s-is-now-open-for-business/?fbclid=IwAR25EQjTxQkeZnQKPkDBXX4E-11hU0LnzdqcqsUpbFQ7lYx8ks9U6Jo6EkU, accessed 2 February 2021

[9] Larkspur Conservation - Conserving Land Through A Revival of Traditional Burial Practices, http://www.larkspurconservation.org, accessed 4 August 2020

[10] Seeker, "Our Decomposing Bodies Are Altering Earth's Chemistry," https://www.seeker.com/earth/our-decomposing-bodies-are-altering-earths-chemistry, accessed 4 August 2020

CPSIA information can be obtained
at www.ICGtesting.com
Printed in the USA
LVHW080917060622
720576LV00003B/14